THE RELUCTANT TWITCHER

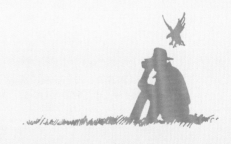

THE RELUCTANT TWITCHER

A *Quite* Truthful Account of My Big Birding Year

Richard Pope

Foreword by Graeme Gibson

NATURAL HERITAGE BOOKS
A MEMBER OF THE DUNDURN GROUP
TORONTO

Published by Natural Heritage Books, a member of the Dundurn Group

Copy Editor: Allison Hirst
Designer: Jennifer Scott
Printer: Friesens

Library and Archives Canada Cataloguing in Publication

Pope, Richard
    The reluctant twitcher : a quite truthful account of my big birding year / by Richard Pope.

Includes index.
ISBN 978-1-55488-458-2

    1. Pope, Richard. 2. Birds--Ontario. 3. Bird watching--Ontario--Humor. 4. Bird watchers--Canada--Biography. I. Title.

QL677.5.P66 2009   598.072'34713   C2009-902460-8

1   2   3   4   5   13   12   11   10   09

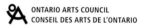

We acknowledge the support of the **Canada Council for the Arts** and the **Ontario Arts Council** for our publishing program. We also acknowledge the financial support of the **Government of Canada** through the **Book Publishing Industry Development Program** and **The Association for the Export of Canadian Books**, and the **Government of Ontario** through the **Ontario Book Publishers Tax Credit program**, and the **Ontario Media Development Corporation**.

Care has been taken to trace the ownership of copyright material used in this book. The author and the publisher welcome any information enabling them to rectify any references or credits in subsequent editions.

J. Kirk Howard, President

Printed and bound in Canada.
www.dundurn.com

Dundurn Press	Gazelle Book Services Limited	Dundurn Press
3 Church Street, Suite 500	White Cross Mills	2250 Military Road
Toronto, Ontario, Canada	High Town, Lancaster, England	Tonawanda, NY
M5E 1M2	LA1 4XS	U.S.A. 14150

*This book is dedicated to the memory of my
father and great friend, Ernie Pope, and to the
memory of Charlie Molony and Ott Devitt*

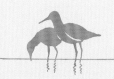

Contents

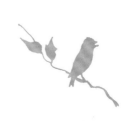

List of Illustrations and Photographs

Grasshopper Sparrow.
Sam Barone   38

Blackpoll Warbler (male).
Barry S. Cherriere   44

Mourning Warbler (male).
Sam Barone   52

Hermit Thrush.
Carol M. Horner   54

Black-backed Woodpecker (male).
Andrew Don   59

American Three-toed Woodpecker (male).
Mark Peck   60

Spruce Grouse (male).
Andrew Don   62

Barrow's Goldeneye (male).
Jean Iron   66

Snowy Owl.
Jean Iron   68

Illustrations and Photographs

Illustrations and Photographs

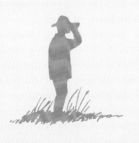

Foreword

WITH EACH NEW REVELATION about our human assault on Nature, more people become birdwatchers. Richard Pope's observation that there are now over fifty million bird enthusiasts in Canada and the United States alone is remarkable. However, it doesn't seem out of line when you consider that BirdLife International's Global Partnership has 2.5 million members and ten million active supporters.

It didn't used to be like that. When I started out, more than forty years ago, birdwatchers were pictured as an eccentric minority wearing odd hats, sensible raingear, and sturdy shoes: a nutty kind of tribe united by an inexplicable enthusiasm for birds. It was this fusty image that prompted some Audubon enthusiasts in the 1950s to describe themselves as "birders," so as not to be mistaken for wimpy oddballs. Ironically, early birdwatchers had chosen their name specifically to distinguish themselves from traditional "birders," who were commercial bird-catchers, or fowlers; in some places a wild cat was also called a "birder."

It was Rachael Carson's 1962 book *Silent Spring* that first focused public attention on birds. Its enormous success and influence is credited with inspiring one of the first public outcries over pesticides, pollution, and environmental destruction. Carson's readers began to recognize that birds in general played the same role on earth as the proverbial canaries did in coal mines. Which is to say, in dying they warned the miners.

Humans were fascinated by birds long before we'd begun to threaten their continued existence. We came to consciousness as a species surrounded by them, when they would have been present in unimaginable numbers. As late as 1866, a legendary flight of Passenger Pigeons was recorded in Southern Ontario. More than a mile wide, with an estimated two birds to the square yard, it took fourteen hours to pass overhead. There were an estimated three billion birds in that assemblage. Nor was it just Passenger Pigeons whose flights darkened the sky: Eskimo Curlews and Golden Plover also gathered in enormous flocks. John James Audubon reports that forty-eight thousand of the latter were gunned down one day near New Orleans.

It isn't difficult to imagine the sense of wonder that our distant forebears felt in the presence of birds. Apparently free from the dictates of gravity, birds soared easily on the wind.

Hunter-gatherers moving laboriously over the land must have envied the freedom with which birds flew on ahead, much in the same way as we do now when watching them from a traffic jam. In *Grass, Sky, Song*, Trevor Herriot describes how the indigenous Siouan people, the Lakota, Dakota, and Nakota, believed that the holy is "the air flowing within and around all living things. As masters of the realm that is the source of spirit and the medium of all spiritual transactions, all birds are spiritual teachers and messengers …" Or as we find it in Ecclesiastes: "A bird of the air shall carry the voice, and that which hath wings shall tell the matter."

Although birds hover near the centre of most mythologies and religions, there are very few, if any, of them in Hell. From the Christian dove to Quetzalcoatl (the Aztec plumed serpent), and from Raven Man to Plato's description of the soul growing wings and feathers, birds are generally associated with creativity and the human soul, with the spiritual communications between the gods and man.

At the same time, there's something very personal in our relationship with birds. As I've noted elsewhere, a great many birdwatchers — from those who simply maintain feeders in their gardens to those who wander the world in search of new, often more exotic species — have stumbled onto a seductive truth: paying attention to birds is being mindful of Life itself. We birders seldom think of our pursuit this clearly, but sometimes, unexpectedly, we are overtaken by a sense of wonder and gratitude. Surely it is the encounter with a force much larger than ourselves that moves us.

Their omnipresence, along with the richness and variety of both species and numbers, helps to explain why we relate to birds in such remarkably varied ways. Pigeon fanciers race them, while others develop exotic breeds of roosters out of what was once a Jungle Fowl. There are fighting cocks, caged singing birds, and parrots who speak languages other than their own. I once gave my partner a pair of Peacocks for her birthday, which in retrospect seems a peculiar thing to have done. Thirty-five million pheasants are bred each year in Britain for the gun — far more than could ever be eaten, thus confirming there are still many among us who find it amusing to kill. In contrast, a ravaged old woman regularly feeds stale bread to gangs of pigeons, Ring-billed Gulls, and sparrows at the edge of a parking lot around the corner from my house. Smiling beatifically with pigeons on her shoulders and gulls between her boots, she might be St. Francis returned as a bag lady.

Finally, of course, there are birdwatchers and/or birders, many of whom are fiercely competitive, both with themselves and others. I once travelled with a fellow whose preoccupation with shorebirds and waders made him utterly scornful of the "dickey-birds" living in the forest. Nevertheless, I suspect most bird enthusiasts simply maintain well-stocked feeders and bird baths, conducive to a more relaxed form of watching, though an increasing number go a step farther and contribute information about population trends by acting as volunteers at field stations, or by recording their sightings for projects such as Feeder Watch or the annual Canadian Lakes Loon Survey.

True amateurs have made a hugely important contribution to our knowledge of birds and their behaviour.

I first met Richard Pope because of our shared enthusiasm for Pelee Island and its birds. Just off the tip of the more celebrated point of the same name, Pelee Island is a great place to welcome passage migrants. The local community hosts a SpringSong Festival in May, the focus of which is a bird race in which teams strive to see as many species as possible in a twenty-four hour period. A unique feature of this event is that competitors cannot use any form of motorized vehicle in their search. The winners and runners-up are celebrated at a banquet on the Saturday night.

Over the years, Richard and I have often found ourselves wandering about together in search of a reported Yellow-breasted Chat, an Acadian Flycatcher, or perhaps the Prothonotary Warbler. I must say that Richard's patience and persistence is humbling; he often remains in the gathering dusk well after I've abandoned the search. Thus, I wasn't surprised to learn that he'd committed himself to seeing three hundred species in Ontario, during what birders call a Big Year.

We humans seem to need challenges. In the realm of birds and birdwatchers, these challenges are generally focused on "listing," or keeping a record of all the birds seen in a day, a year, a life and/or in a backyard or a bird race on an island. The considerable challenge that Richard set himself was nothing more than a marginally insane extension of Pelee's Green Bird Race, except that he was mostly racing against himself. Or perhaps against the void that would have probably loomed, were he not to have achieved his goal of three hundred species.

All races are against time. The birds themselves are racing time during their migration. Too soon or too late and they'll die or be unable to breed. So, in his counting and his self-imposed time-limit, Richard Pope is in some ways imitating Nature itself. His engaging account of his Big Year could well be called One Man's Migration.

Finally, I ask myself: How much easier would it have been to achieve Richard's goal forty years ago? And how much harder will it be to count three hundred species during a year in Ontario thirty years from now. Will it even be possible?

GRAEME GIBSON

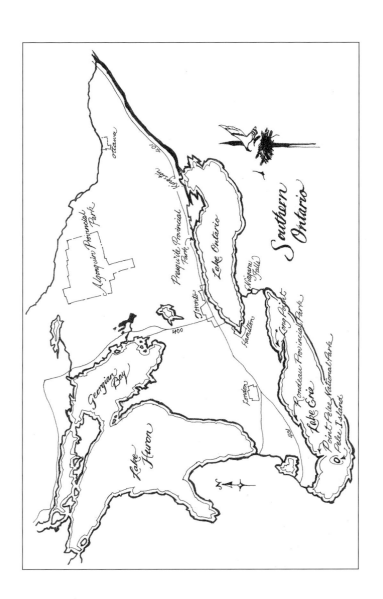

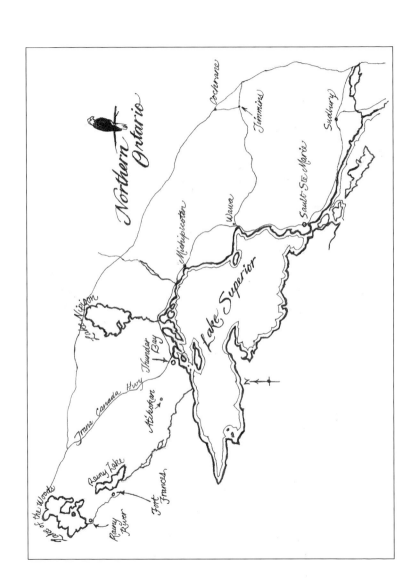

Northern Ontario

Lake Superior

Cochrane
Timmins
Sudbury
Sault Ste. Marie
Wawa
Michipicoten
Lake Nipigon
Thunder Bay
Atikokan
Trans Canada Hwy
Rainy Lake
Lake of the Woods
Rainy River
Fort Frances

Twitch Not Lest Ye Be Twitched.

— THE MINOR PROPHETS

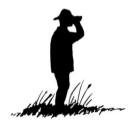

It's a tick.

— HUGH CURRIE

Preface

To twitch, or not to twitch — that is the question.

— Henry IX, Act 77

"Pope is strictly for the birds," say some thoughtless wags, without stopping to consider why this might be so. My fateful connection with birds predates my birth. On a star-crossed morning in May of 1941, my father, Ernie, and two friends, Charlie Molony and Ott Devitt, went to King City to investigate a Pileated Woodpecker's nest in a farmer's woodlot — a relatively harmless thing to do. This was before drugs and switch knives became the fashionable way for young men to spend a spring morning.

They took my mother with them, which was not unusual, except that she was some five months pregnant and her running skills were compromised by this fact. On the way back across the field the group was distracted by the crazed bellowing and clod-throwing antics of an enraged Jersey bull, which for some reason had taken umbrage at the invasion of his turf and was going ballistic. Mother, not a bull-lover at the best of times, was scared witless. There was but one tree in the field, a superannuated white pine, and the men somehow got my mother into the tree even though she was not what you would call a natural climber. Fear may have helped her. The bull charged and the men, too, got up the tree with an uncomfortably small grace period. An hour later the bull lost interest and wandered off looking for someone else to terrify. That's what they do; it's their thing.

It was some time before the men, armed with stones and a disconcertingly minuscule amount of bravado, were able to coax my mother down from the tree to make a run for the fence. And run my mother did, certain the bull was in hot pursuit the whole way. Even later in life she never recalled the episode dispassionately.

Leaving aside my unnatural attraction to Pileated Woodpeckers — my first "heard only" bird — and my incapacitating fear of all bulls, especially, but not exclusively Jerseys, let us rather note that in this episode we see the origin of the connection between me and birds. I never made a choice to become a birder. The gods willed it. They even make me fly frequently in my dreams. It can be exhausting.

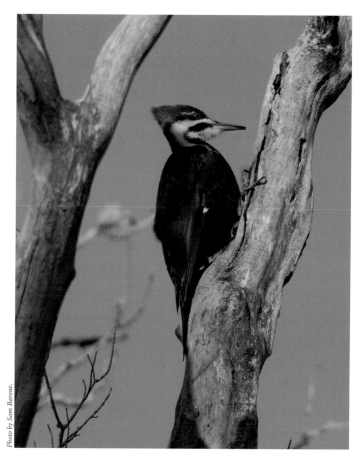

Photo by Sam Barone.

Pileated Woodpecker (male). Algonquin Provincial Park. The red moustachial stripe indicates this bird is a male.

Birding, as is widely known, is the fastest growing pastime in the Western world with well over fifty million participants in Canada and the United States alone. It has grown in quantum leaps since 2001. It is reported that 53,350,000 Americans feed wild birds (2006 National Survey of Fishing, Hunting, and Wildlife-Associated Recreation; report by the U.S. Fish and Wildlife Service). Throw in the Canadians and we're over fifty-five million! People become birdwatchers (slightly less serious) or birders (slightly more serious and sometimes approaching the manic; occasionally called "bird nerds" behind their backs, a term I shall henceforth eschew in this book) because birds are beautiful, numerous, and varied, and often available in one's own backyard. In colder climes, many people gaze mindlessly out their back windows all day long for up to six months of the year. Most mornings in May one can find people, like my friends George Fairfield and John Carley, crouched in the half darkness on their back porches staring intently off into the distance, patrolling for loons. They are part of Loon Watch. I leave you to draw your own conclusions, but tell me you don't know someone like that. What is not known is what occasionally pushes a relatively normal birder over the brink and turns him or her into a twitcher.

What exactly *is* a twitcher, you might ask. The big *Oxford English Dictionary* defines it as "an instrument for clinching hog-rings." This is not a meaning I favour. The porcine allusion seems quite superfluous. The *Concise Oxford Dictionary* defines it as "a birdwatcher who tries to get sightings of rare birds," but also "a person or thing that twitches." Though I use the term in this book in the first sense, you might be surprised how often the two meanings overlap. Twitchers range from the merely utterly possessed and driven to the certifiably insane, ready to kill without hesitation to see a real rarity. British twitchers have been known to abandon spouses at the altar to rush off to the Scilly Isles for some off-course migrant. The Scillies, not surprisingly, are known for their twitchers.

I am told there are some who might not even know what a Big Year is, hard to believe as this seems. A Big Year is a term widely used in the birding confraternity to describe the attempt to see some improbably high number of birds in a prescribed place in a single year. It can be any place — South Dakota, Nunavut, Rhode Island — downtown Moose Jaw for that matter.

I did my Big Year in Ontario, Canada, where the gold standard is to try to see three hundred birds in a year. It's not impossible, but it involves a lot of running around. Ontario is four times the size of Texas. Someone phones and says there's a possible Dovekie in Cornwall, so you whip off to Cornwall. Just after failing to find the Dovekie, you check the Internet in your cheap motel room with the cigarette burns on the bedspread and the pair of stalk eyes peering out of the sinkhole and learn there is an illusive Sprague's Pipit in Rainy River. Rainy River is exactly two thousand kilometres from Cornwall. You get the picture. You spend a lot of time in a car trying to figure out how to make things all right again with your family. Next time, if there is one, I may well try downtown Moose Jaw: Moosejavians, beware!

At 2:20 p.m. on October 24, 2007, while I was in my car — where else? — in hot pursuit of some bird I failed to see, it suddenly occurred to me that I should write up my Big Year in book form. Others have done so, in the United States, England, Australia, and possibly Burundi, probably with huge commercial success. Why not me? I did not stop to remember Graeme Gibson's lament that he was turned down by at least thirty-six publishers before getting one to seriously consider his wonderful *The Bedside Book of Birds*. I began my book that very evening after half a bottle of excellent California Zinfandel — 16.5 percent, if I recall correctly, possibly 17 percent; a "big zin" in any case. The result awaits you.

A portion of the revenues generated by this book will go to the Toronto Ornithological Club, the Pelee Island Bird Observatory, and the Ontario Field Ornithologists. BUY THIS BOOK. Give a copy to your mother, or if you have friends, to one or both of them.

And when you're out on the trail, mind you don't get between ol' Poper and a Kentucky Warbler.

1

I Am Committed

The Horror! The Horror!

— JOSEPH CONRAD, *HEART OF DARKNESS*

NO, NOT COMMITTED AS YOU understand it. That may come soon. They are after me, but they have not caught me yet and I am, to the contrary, still very much at large. But doing a Big Year frequently leads to being binned, so your thinking may not be too far off the mark. Big Years not uncommonly lead to increasingly bizarre behaviour and a steep descent into full-blown lunacy. The word *loon* inescapably comes to mind.

If ever temptation to do such a year should beckon, banish it immediately, my friends; failing that, for heaven's sake, keep it secret. Under no circumstances should you mention it to any-body, particularly a friend.

I, myself, you see, not only did not want to do a Big Year, but never even had the thought cross my mind. But often dur-ing 2006, my birding buddy Hugh Currie would say, "Now that you're going to be retired, you should do a Big Year in 2007."

Every year is a Big Year for old Hughie, twitcher extraor-dinaire. I ignored these unwanted suggestions. I was not a twitcher, had no interest in becoming one, and secretly consid-ered such people rather odd.

Finally, one day, to get him off the topic of my doing a Big Year, I off-handedly replied to his overture: "Yeah, I guess I should." Meaning, of course, that yes, I *should*, even though I, in fact, *will not*. I never thought about it again.

In late December I had to go to England and only returned on January 11. On the twelfth, I happened to be talking to John Carley, a fellow member of the Toronto Ornithological Club, who "innocently" asked me how my Big Year was going.

"What Big Year?" I asked in horror.

"You're doing a Big Year this year because you're retired."

"I am? Who told you that?"

"Hugh announced it at the last meeting of the club. Every-one knows."

Oh, my God.

I began thinking like mad. How can I get out of this? I don't want to rush around like a madman. I just like poking around at my own speed, checking out the local birds when I feel like it. I don't need constant rarities. I actually like common birds. Though I would never tell anybody, unless being broken on a Catherine wheel, I even like Blue Jays. Yes, I know they can be "bad actors," but I like them all the same. They have character.

I used to have a little birding group and the older ladies loved me. They all turned out for my bird walks and asked questions about the sparrows, chickadees, and jays. Once, they organized a little get-together at one of their homes so we could all admire the baby Chipping Sparrows in the nest outside the hostess's kitchen window. Just my luck, moments before I arrived a Blue Jay swooped in and devoured all four nestlings

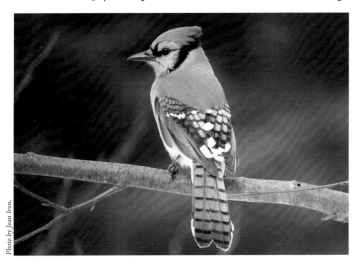

Photo by Jean Iron.

Blue Jay. Algonquin Park. Though aggressive, noisy, and fond of baby birds, Blue Jays are gorgeous creatures.

rapid-fire, and apparently with untoward gusto, before any of the horrified ladies could rush out and save the day.

I had some trouble explaining this one, I can tell you. No suitable apology for the now reviled Blue Jay was forthcoming. I spoke at some length about the beautiful plumage, but they weren't having any of that. I ended up taking the path of least resistance and admitting that the Blue Jay was a nasty, even depraved, avian. But secretly I still liked them, and I do to this day. Sure they can be "bad actors" when viewed anthropomorphically, but then what bird can't? The ladies all loved to watch the Turkey Vultures circling lazily high above on the thermals. But did I tell them why the vultures have bald heads? Or mention their breath? Get serious. Why turn them against yet another species.

Anyway, I suddenly realized I was going to have to look at a lot more than Blue Jays and other commoners if I was going to do a Big Year. My serene existence as a non-entity was shattered. I would have to become an entity, a somebody — and not just in muffler shops like before. Could I live up to it? I knew I had to.

Away with abject thoughts of failure, deep humiliation, and possible physical beating. No more brooding upon my bleak lot. Maybe for once I'd get lucky. I might even find a few really good birds. Imagine if I found Ontario's first Spangled Drongo! They might even name it after me — *Drongo ontariensis popei*. I'd be famous.

Damn it all! I'll show them. I'll throw down the gauntlet.

I am committed.

Let the drama begin.

2

The Pecking Order

For fools rush in where angels fear to tread.

— ALEXANDER POPE, *ESSAY ON CRITICISM*

NOW PEOPLE ARE REALLY GOING to hate me. Who am I to do a Big Year? People hate pretension.

"I wonder what makes Pope think *he* should do a Big Year."

"Who cares what Pope sees?"

"Pope's a geek."

"Who the hell is Pope?"

Joy birding is out. Now I really have to worry about mis-identifications — one or two on the Internet and you're dead meat. One mistake in the field and some bloody rookies are going to start thinking they're better than you. One in front of an expert and it's all over. Your reputation will be in tatters. That's why I like to study each bird, not just take a glance at it and go off half-cocked, though this, too, can backfire.

One day I'm having a very nice time by myself on a country roadside scoping an obliging Grasshopper Sparrow on top of a mullein — really studying the bird. The bird has no forehead at all, and what a nice little white eye-ring. I am happy, confident, on top of my game. There aren't many of these sparrows around today and I'm glad to find one. I feel good about it. You want a scarce bird, old Poper'll find it for you.

A car pulls to a stop behind me and someone gets out. Darn. I keep my eye to the scope. Maybe the person will go away.

"Got something good there?" a voice asks. A treacherous question.

My answer will, of course, depend on who is asking. If it's someone I'm better than, I can say, "it's a Grasshopper Sparrow" and start lecturing on field marks. But if it's Glenn Coady or someone, you don't want him to think you consider the Grasshopper Sparrow a good bird. What to do?

I glance over and my blood runs cold. Oh, my God, I can't believe it. It's Kenn Kaufman! I've seen his picture in books. I should have stuck to solitaire. I was quite good at it.

I must at all costs not let Kaufman think I am bogus. "You mean, you don't want Kaufman to *know* you are bogus, you fraud," says an unpleasant voice. My confidence is sinking fast. It's too late to run for my car.

"What have you got?" asks Kaufman again, cleverly concealing deep underlying malice and suspicion.

I fight back a panic attack. My Grasshopper Sparrow suddenly seems piddling and uninteresting. I could say I had a Brambling or a Fieldfare but it has just flown way off out of sight impossibly far away and has been hit by a Goshawk, but would he buy it?

I blurt out the truth. "Nothing at all, really. Just an ol' Grasshopper Sparrow. I saw him on the fence and decided to check him out."

"They seem to be extremely common here," says Kaufman in mock innocence. "I've had forty six in the last quarter mile."

I'm tempted to say, "Is that all?" but instead I say, "Yeah, they're almost garbage birds around here. I'm seeing them, like, everywhere."

"No bird is a garbage bird," says Kaufman sternly.

I am racked with contrition. I despise the term myself. I only used it to impress him and make him think they were nothing to me, but now instead I've made him hate me worse. And I so wanted to get off on the right foot.

I glance at him and by mistake I make eye contact. I see what he's thinking and it's terrible. I feel like I'm before the Truth and Reconciliation Committee, only with no hope of reconciliation. It's like looking into the eyes of Desmond Tutu. I want to fall on my knees and embrace his shins and tell him I am a fraud and a shyster. I may even mention the Crispy Crunch I stole in 1947, though I've spent a whole life paying for it in guilt.

Kaufman begins to shift from foot to foot. He is watching my eyes. He fears he may be dealing with a madman. "Let's see your bird," he says.

For the first time, I suddenly realize that it might not even *be* a Grasshopper Sparrow. What if it's a female House Sparrow or an antshrike or something? Oh, God, if only it would fly away. What's the matter with it? Is it stuck to the top of that mullein or something? I sneeze loudly. The bird hangs tough. I have a coughing fit. I try to knock my scope down into the poison ivy, but Kaufman is onto it like a jungle cat. How long, oh Lord, how long?

"Thanks," I say. "Clumsy bugger, aren't I?"

"I do it all the time, but don't worry. I'll put the bird back in your scope for you pronto."

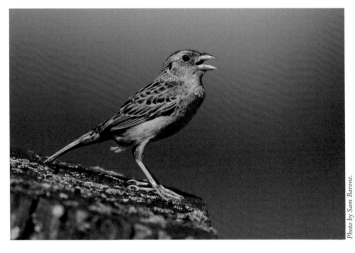

Grasshopper Sparrow. Carden Alvar. Foreheads do not come flatter.

38

Nos morituri te salutamus, I say to myself — We who are about to die salute you.

Kaufman stares at the bird. "You dirty, lying snake," he says.

Well, it sounds like, "Oh, that *is* a nice Grasshopper," but I understand his true meaning. Oh, yes. Don't think I don't. He smiles. I search the corners of his lips for faint quivering — the sure sign of fighting back an incipient sneer.

"You wouldn't know a Grasshopper Sparrow from a watermelon," he continues, masking his speech under the English sounds for "I really like the little guys." But I am a linguist and understand him, even though he tries to encrypt his speech.

"Bogusness is rife," I say to him. "Forgive, forgive, Master."

Perhaps if I tear off my shirt and hurl myself down into the poison ivy, maybe stuff a couple of handfuls of leaves down my craw, he'll let me off.

"Thanks for the look," replies Kaufman.

"I do a lot of work with orphans," I say feebly.

As he turns to leave, he sticks out his hand and says, "The name's Kennn."

"Kenn?" I say.

"No, Kennn. I'm Albanian. Enver Kennn. Just started birding. The Grasshopper's a lifer for me today."

"You mean you're not …"

Suddenly I recall that Kenn Kaufman is dark, bearded, tall, and lean — something along the Lesser Yellowlegs line. This guy is blondish and clean-shaven, shorter and more heavy-set — closer to the Dunlin style. I could have been lording it over him the entire time. I am just about to review the field marks of the Grasshopper Sparrow for the guy, when I suddenly understand the deception. Dunlin. Dunnlin. This is all part of some bizarre test. No, of course it isn't Kenn Kaufman. Nor is it Enver Kennn. It's Jon Dunn! Kaufman has sent him here to sucker me into some minor descriptive error. If he asks me anything about the remiges, I'm outta here in a flash.

I smile weirdly and Dunn suddenly makes a break for his car. Probably going for his laptop to spread the truth on "Birders' Exposé" — THIS JUST IN. POPE ENTIRELY BOGUS.

"Funny little tail, eh?" I cry out as he speeds away. "Nice breast!"

Oh, dear. I hope Dunn didn't think there was anything odd about me.

I am devastated, but I see the lesson in all this. I must be super careful all year lest my enemies rejoice. Make it hard for those who loathe pretension to expose me — earn my place in the pecking order, so to speak. Better a pecker than a peckee.

So much for stress-free birding.

3

The Rules

Scooby wee WEEtee zitZEEzer chup chup dooby oowah

— CROCKMAN'S SPARROW

PERHAPS, I THINK NAIVELY, SINCE I don't even really want to do a Big Year, people will at least cut me some slack and show some understanding.

"Going for 339, eh?" says Carley, pandering to my worst fears. So much for understanding. Three hundred and thirty-eight is the magical record number for a Big Year in Ontario achieved by Glenn Coady in 1996. They say it will never be equalled, let alone beaten, and I do not doubt it. I am appalled that someone might think I even want to beat it. I'd kill myself if I got to 337. All I hope to do is have a little fun, chase a few birds, and try to see three hundred in the year. But now if I come in with a mere three hundred or so, I will still be seen as a failure and loser. Oh dear, oh dear.

Well, I reckon, if people know about it, I am at least going to lay down some clear ground rules. I decide all I want to do is *see* three hundred birds in 2007. Innocent though this seems, this turns out to be a problem. Imagine that pretentious wannabe Pope wanting to *see* three hundred birds and not count birds only heard. Who does he think he is? The American Birding Association (ABA) says one is to count heard-only birds to cut down on unnecessary harassment. Pope will be going around driving birds insane with huge tape recorders and ghetto blasters and dragging chains through marshes, crushing infant Yellow Rails just to get to *see* one. I already hate him, the dirty rail-maimer.

But I stick to my guns. I make rules not to kill, maim, or even disfigure any rails, even adults; to use tapes sparingly; and to almost never indulge in any kind of harassing behaviour — even when no one is looking.

Don't get me wrong, though. I thoroughly approve of the ABA decision to accept heard-only birds. Anything that cuts down on harassment of birds is to the good. Birds are already in enough trouble as it is without further danger from the people that love them — and I don't just mean the Red Knot. Anyone who does not think birds are on the ropes should immediately read Bridget Stutchbury's excellent *Silence of the Songbirds* and prepare to weep.

I want to *see* my birds because I know that identification of birds in the field by song can be very tricky even for the best ears. And sadly, I no longer have the best of ears. I discovered this a few years ago when we were walking along a trail and my wife, Felicity, said, "What was that?"

"What was what?" I replied.

"That loud, insistent song we just heard."

Fifty feet down the trail I heard a faint song and said, "Oh, *that*. That's a Bay-breasted Warbler."

I still remember the thrill several springs ago at Rondeau Provincial Park when I heard a Blackpoll Warbler for the first time in years. Felicity and I were waiting patiently, fifty feet apart on the bridge on the Tulip Tree Trail, for the Prothonotary Warbler to fly in, when suddenly I heard a Blackpoll.

"Dear! Dear!" I yelled jubilantly. "A miracle has happened. I hear a Blackpoll. Over the winter I must have reacquired my high range hearing. Cape Mays beware! Grasshopper Sparrows, don't even try to fool me. Poper is back!" I began madly glassing the towering silver maple tops. "I can't find it," I called. "Wonder where it is. Can you see it from where you are? It's up pretty high."

"It's not that thing right above your head, is it?" asked Felicity, pointing.

I looked up, and four metres above my head on a drooping branch hung a Blackpoll Warbler singing his heart out. I was thrilled. It was good news that I could still hear them, crescendo and all. So what if they have to be five metres away or closer. You can't have everything. You learn to adjust and use

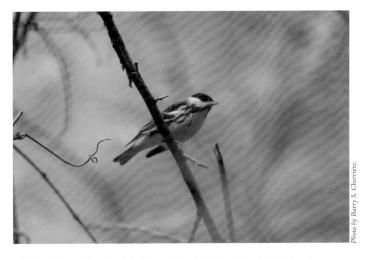

Photo by Barry S. Cherriere.

Blackpoll Warbler (male). Point Pelee National Park. Having just completed the longest migration of any wood warbler, this bird is resting quietly.

AAAA — automatic auditory avian adjustment. For example, if I hear a Grasshopper Sparrow now, I know just where to look — beside or under my feet. I don't waste time looking way out on the periphery like some poor rubes.

One day, while standing beside a barbed-wire fence in knee-deep poison ivy waiting to see a Loggerhead Shrike, I foolishly mentioned my incipient hearing loss to Glenn Coady, who was being driven mad by the myriad Grasshopper Sparrows singing six fields away. Coady was horrified. "I'd kill myself if that happened to me," he said. That really made me feel good. It was clear that this was what any real birder would do. It was equally clear that to establish myself in his eyes, I would now have to off myself or he'd think I was bogus for sure. I was in a tough spot — no traffic, no deep rivers, nothing. And I was unarmed. I briefly considered throwing myself onto the barbed-wire fence or trying to get my neck wrapped in it or something, but if I only managed a half job — a maiming or something — Coady would really hate me. I thought it over and decided to wait until I'd finished the year. Maybe I could acquire a gun or a phial of poison or contact Rent-a-Krait in the interim. In the short term, I'd have to do the best I could and learn to cover my tracks.

Oh, birding by ear gives one an enormous advantage, no question of that, and although it helps to minimize warbler neck, it does have its limitations. Sometimes a bird does only part of his song and sounds like another bird. Often they sing just variations, not theme. And everyone hears birds differently.

One day I'm out with a novice and he says, "What made that *weedly queedly?*"

"What *weedly queedly?*" I ask.

"There, that *weedly queedly*," he says.

"Oh, *that*. That's a Blue Jay," I say. "I had no idea what you meant. It's not saying *weedly queedly*, but *queedly weedly*."

"It's clearly saying *weedly queedly*," he says.

"*Queedly weedly*."

"*Weedly frigging queedly*."

"*Queedly weedly*," I insist, refusing to back down.

Such things often end badly. Only the arrival of several cherubic oldsters keen to nail their first Blue Jay forestalls the fisticuffs that so often ensue in such situations.

The National Geographic *Field Guide to the Birds of North America* says that the Eastern Bluebird sings *chur chur-lee chur-lee*. *The Sibley Guide to Birds* says it sings *chiti WEEW wewidoo*. My friend Bob Carswell, poor fellow, thinks it sounds like "Peter, Paul and Mary." Of course, in actual fact, it says "Vercingetorix," a clear tribute to the famous Gallic leader who so valiantly opposed Julius Caesar, though, admittedly, there are those who fail to hear it this way. Sibley lists the red Fox Sparrow as singing *weet weeto teeoo teeo tzee tzer zezer reep*. This is amazing, since if you listen carefully, the bird, at least the northern ones, quite clearly sings,

> I see
>> I see
>>> *keeky*
>>> I see a ^*bird.*

Sometimes song description is merely a reflection of the depravity of the listener. It has been claimed (note that I do not mention Fred Bodsworth's name) that the White-crowned Sparrow does not say, "Poor Jojo missed his bus," but, "Poor Jojo pissed his pants." Still more disgusting, the *Nuthatch Aid to Birdsong Identification*, designed and written by Antonio Salvadori, claims Kirtland's Warbler sings, "Fel-ic-ity-has-to-wee-wee," something so rude I have not even mentioned it to my wife, who would not be amused; nor, of course, am I.

Many birds sing or can sing overlapping songs. I think of Margaret's story of the Yellow Warbler, which perfectly mastered the Prairie Warbler's song and fooled everybody. And you have to be good to fool Margaret. She does chips. I have been fooled and seen experts fooled by Yellow Warblers doing their Chestnut-sided Warbler song, by lazy Red-eyed Vireos and vigorous Blue-headed Vireos, and by Pine Warblers, Worm-eating Warblers, and Dark-eyed Juncos trilling at uncharacteristic speeds and pitches. I once saw a lowly Chipping Sparrow fly into a patch of marsh grass, and watched as numerous expert birders dismissed its song as that of a Swamp Sparrow doing its faster call. Put it this way, if bird identification by song was certain, why did the new *Atlas of the Breeding Birds of Ontario* not accept Yellow-billed Cuckoos unless they were seen? Birds can and do learn each other's songs. I rest my case.

The point is, if you rely solely on sound and get lazy with your eyes, you will miss some birds and may misidentify a few others.

Lord knows, birding by sight can be tricky enough. Just read Kenn Kaufman's *Advanced Birding* if you don't agree. I have a friend who had to be tranquilized because of recurrent nightmares featuring Kaufman's chart, "Bills of *Empidonax* Flycatchers as seen from below." There are enough problems with bird identification even when you see them. I'm going to try to see *and* hear as many of my birds as possible, no matter how long it takes.

Margaret Bain and Hugh Currie, my main accomplices, try to be understanding. They see me as some kind of holy fool. When we meet people in the field, they both quickly explain that "of course, Richard is trying to *see* three hundred birds this year. He's a purist." They mean nutter, and this is certainly how people take it. But I hang tough.

Not only do I hang tough on seeing my birds, but I decide I will only count birds I see well. I want only birds I am certain of and have identified beyond a shadow of doubt. None of this standing on the tip of Point Pelee and hearing Alan Wormington or Tom Hince or Pete Read yell, "Juvenile Dickcissel," and looking up to see a distant speck flying madly back to the United States and then checking Dickcissel on my list that evening. No, I want to try to find and positively identify as many of the birds as I can myself, though this is not a rule. Phone tips and postings on Ontbirds are fine, and counting birds Margaret or Hugh or someone else sees first is okay, but I have to get a really good diagnostic look. I don't want to have Ron Pittaway ask me what the tertial fringing was like on my juvenile Ruff and have to say, "Duh." Nor do I want to end up like Joey Slinger, who has made something of a career out of trying to convince clandestine doubters and sniggerers that he really did see a Curlew Sandpiper where everyone else failed. Though I have no doubts about what Slinger saw, I want only birds that no one can doubt on my list.

People say, "He's some kind of whacko purist, that Pope." But I'm only doing it for fun and personal satisfaction, and what fun is it to have a list full of soft birds? I want a clean, hard list. That's a rule. I mention it to Ron Pittaway and he entirely agrees.

So there.

4

Pish and Chips

Chip.

— MEANINGFUL SOUND HEARD IN THE BUSHES.

THIS IS NOT A CHAPTER on the culinary aspect of birding and birders' favourite meals. It is a technical chapter dealing with two aspects of birding crucial to anyone hoping to do a Big Year or break some record.

First, pishing. There are, of course, those who call it *shpishing*. If you say *pish pish pish* and ignore the initial *pi*, it sounds like you are saying *shpish shpish*. Which is correct? It is an unresolvable ontological conundrum, so let us just call it pishing and get on with it.

Those who do not number among the cognoscenti may not have a firm grasp of the meaning of the term. Pishing is what you do when you walk along a path and a bird suddenly flashes into sight and goes to ground before you are able to get a decent look. You wait. Nothing. You wait longer. Nothing. Birds are patient. It could be napping. How can you make it show itself, however briefly? This is where pishing comes into play. You purse your lips and blow air through them, going *pish pish pish* and, theoretically, the bird will pop up to see what is going on and you will be able to identify it.

Of course, it doesn't always work this way. Some birds are pish-resistant and require prolonged pishing; others are simply unpishable.

Often it is a matter of technique. I am not a good pisher. On occasion I have pished a pishable bird long and steadily only to have it hang tough in the bushes, refusing even to twitch. Then some really skilled pisher, like Dean Ware, comes along, utters one little pish, and the bird, stunned by my level of incompetence, pops up as if it were on a string. Ware's pishing, squeaking, and whistling are so irritating that no bird can resist; you only hope the bird comes up quickly. Volume and timbre enter into it. Sometimes the quietest little pish is all it takes; other times it can take half a pint of saliva and a beach towel. You have to be ready to experiment and hope your handlers are not there to observe.

In some cases you have to go farther than pishing. I am not talking about well-lobbed stones and mad, kicking rushes into the undergrowth. The ABA no longer sanctions such techniques. I'm talking about hand-kissing. Your own is least dangerous, depending, of course, on how long you have known the person beside you. You simply place your lips on the back of your hand (some purists insist on the back of the knuckles of the second and middle fingers — never the ring finger), purse your lips, and suck air in through your teeth. It can drive 'em wild. Other times it leaves them cold, forcing you to fall back on extreme measures such as screech-owl imitation, a technique to be used only circumspectly in the presence of non-birders, particularly those with medical degrees.

Not everyone can do screech-owl imitations. You need hyperactive salivary glands and the ability to roll your tongue and blow over the spit while holding your lips in a special position. Some can manage the trill; few do a good whinny.

I tried to learn. Oh, yes, I tried. Don't think I didn't. But like the soft *r* in Russian, I was never able to learn the sound. At the Russian School at Middlebury College in 1965, the world's greatest soft *r* expert was called in to teach me how to make a soft *r*. You need the back of your tongue low, the centre arched upwards against the hard palate, and the tip pressed against the lower front teeth; I think the sides are supposed to flutter or something. Anyway, the phonetics specialist attempted to teach me using Popsicle sticks to force my recalcitrant tongue into the correct position. When all was ready, he said, "Okay. Say *r*."

I said "Gaa," just before my gag reflex kicked in and I got a mouthful of splinters from the crushed Popsicle sticks. He was able to retract his fingers just in time. After several weeks

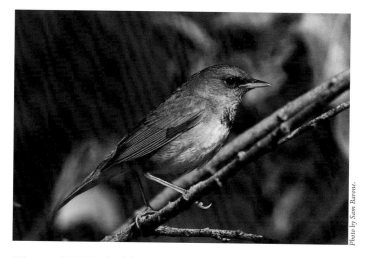

Photo by Sam Barone.

Mourning Warbler (male). Kirkfield. Such stunning skulkers are seldom seen like this.

we gave up on this approach. I had no more success with the screech-owl trill, though I tried everything. A pity; it can be very effective. I have had modest success with the Saw-whet Owl death screech, but it just isn't the same.

The best I ever heard was a fellow named Mike Runtz, though it must be admitted, Dan Bone is no slouch.

We were birding at Pelee and it was slow — real slow, as they say. A Mourning Warbler in Tilden's Woods sang once and shut up. Mike pished him out. He kept on pishing. Nothing more. Then a bit of seductive knuckle kissing produced a White-throated Sparrow and a bit of rustling. Suddenly, Runtz upped the ante and began a screech-owl trill. A Lincoln's Sparrow immediately shot up, crown feathers erect, desperate to locate the enemy. An Eastern Towhee popped up. Runtz kept trilling. A Blue Jay swooped in and began to furiously hop about. Now Runtz began a series of high descending whinnies. The towhee attacked the Blue Jay. Another towhee appeared and joined in. Two more jays shot down and joined the fray. Sparrows began to fly up everywhere. A Carolina Wren appeared, spoiling for a scrap. The Mourning Warbler got out while the going was good. Things were rapidly getting out of hand. Turkey Vultures were circling above in mystified disbelief. An American Crow appeared and began cawing furiously. I was getting nervous. It was turning into an Alfred Hitchcock scene.

Two elderly ladies came by and stood in utter amazement. I attempted an explanatory grin, which may have been taken amiss, since a flicker of real fear appeared on their faces at that very instant. Runtz noticed nothing and turned it up a notch. He was by now in full flight, alternating pishing, kissing, and wild trills. The two ladies hastened down the trail and one produced a cell phone and called 911. I heard her giving exact directions to our location. I tried to speak to Runtz, but he was out of control, as was the avian donnybrook. Cravenly I slipped off and rushed to the Visitor Centre to hide. I don't know how it ended. I did hear sirens but am not sure if they were incidental or not. I hope it ended well, though come to think of it, I haven't seen Mike since. I probably should visit him if I can locate the institution.

Obviously, some ability to pish, at least adequately, is greatly desirable for coaxing out difficult birds when you are trying to run up your numbers. So is the ability to "do" chips.

Chips can be very important. Not fresh hot ones with malt vinegar, ketchup, and lots of salt. No. I'm talking about recognizing chip sounds. You're walking, say, in Jobes' Woods in Presqu'ile Provincial Park, and Doug McRae suddenly and for no apparent reason says, "Hermit Thrush."

"Excuse me?" you respond, lost in reverie.

"Hermit Thrush," repeats McRae. Then it dawns on you that on some subliminal level you perceived one single little chip note a moment ago.

"For sure," you say, hopefully before McRae gets suspicious and thinks not only that you did not know that so-readily-

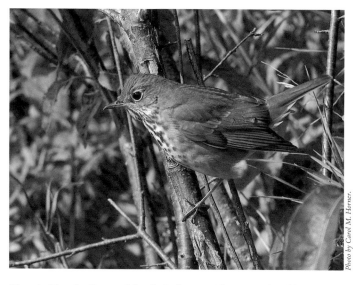

Hermit Thrush. Corner Marsh, Pickering. The rust-red tail betrays this as a Hermit Thrush.

Photo by Carol M. Horner.

recognizable a chip was a Hermit Thrush, but that you may not even have noticed it.

Doing chips is important, especially for identifying skulkers. "A chip is a chip," the foolish might say, but they would be wrong. If you know your chips — forget the songs — you are off to the races. Do not be daunted by the fact that several hundred of the most common chips sound virtually identical to the untrained ear. Be aware that there are bright chips, dull chips, lacklustre chips, "chippy" chips, and so forth. Get a chip recording and start learning them. It will save you an enormous amount of time. And if you misidentify a chip, and pish out a different bird, you can always say, "I guess the Swainson's went the other way or it just isn't going to come out."

I shall not even mention the need to study the recordings of nocturnal migration flight calls because of the concomitant dangers of being mistaken for a street person when lying on your back on the sidewalk at night straining to hear faint overhead calls. This is not for the uninitiated. It can also lead to severe sleep deprivation in migration season. Margaret sleeps every night in May with her window wide open listening for migrating thrushes and can be quite tired by morning.

Suffice it to say that, armed with proper pish and chip skills, your Big Year is going to be a sight easier.

5

Algonquin Grand Slam

How sweet it is!

— ENVER HOXHA

WHEN HUGH SUGGESTS WE KICK off my Big Year with a mid-January trip (January 19–21) to Algonquin Provincial Park, I am all for it. I have already missed almost two weeks by being in England — an inauspicious beginning — and the Razorbill that was so good to me in December 2006 disappeared from Niagara-on-the-Lake just before my return. A quick mid-January trip to Niagara produced ten species of gulls, including California Gull (a first-winter bird in Hamilton), Lesser

Black-backed Gull, and Black-legged Kittiwake, but nothing rare, and I was disappointed. I felt that I desperately needed to get going. American Three-toed Woodpeckers had been showing up in the Park and this is obviously a species not to miss. It becomes one of our five target Algonquin birds.

We decide to spend two nights in Whitney to give us the better part of three days' birding. This turns out to be a smart move. We need the third morning.

Hugh suggests I mention the trip to Margaret to see if she is interested. Margaret, of course, is not about to be left behind. At this point I still firmly believe that she and Hugh are both simply committed to helping me reach three hundred and have no secret intentions of their own to get there ahead of me. The sheer altruism of it all impresses me very favourably. I can't imagine being that selfless.

On Friday morning, January 19, Margaret and Hugh and I leave for Algonquin. We go straight to our motel at Whitney, check in, have lunch, and head for the feeders at the Nature Centre. The feeders are good to us; so is the road. By dark, at 4:45 p.m., I have added seven birds to my year list: Hairy Woodpecker, American Tree Sparrow, Purple Finch, Common Redpoll, Pine Siskin, Evening Grosbeak, and Gray Jay, of which the last species is one of our five target birds. We have also seen many crossbills of both kinds right on the road and are well satisfied, even without our other four targets. None of us know that we will not see redpolls again all winter.

The next morning we get an early start, despite the fact that after breakfast it is still minus thirty degrees Celsius. Though the Centre doesn't officially open until 9:00 a.m., we sneak in a side door and find wild activity at the feeders featuring at least fifty very bold Evening Grosbeaks. Then we go off in serious pursuit of our target birds — Hugh doesn't like to fool around — and by dark we have Black-backed Woodpecker and Boreal Chickadee, both on the Opeongo Road.

The chickadee is easy, but the woodpecker causes some stress. I see it fly across the road in front of me and mark where I think it lands. I plunge in after it across an alder bog and up a steep hill and find it about seventy-five metres back in the bush, busily attacking a spruce tree. I call out "Black-backed" and turn to look for Hugh and see him flailing madly through the alders up to his waist in snow. Trying not to think about heart attacks, I watch him motor up the hill. Thank God the bird is still there.

"Where's Margaret?" I ask.

"I'm down here on the road," comes a little voice on the wind. Suspecting we just might have a good bird when she saw us both suddenly run off the road and plunge into the snow-filled bush, she has come up to see what it is all about. "What have you got?"

"A Black-backed," I say.

"I'll be right up," says Margaret.

"No," I call, "wait there. I'll come down to get you. There's an easier way up." I don't want her wrecking her hip replacement this early in the trip. Save her for the Three-toed, you know. She has great ears.

I find a better way back to the road and break the trail a bit. Margaret plunges in behind me, and all is well until we come

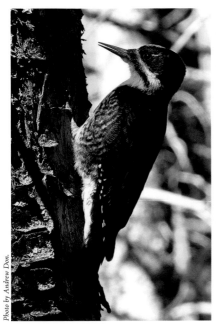

Black-backed Woodpecker (male). Algonquin Provincial Park. Aptly named, this boreal species loves dying spruce.

Photo by Andrew Don.

to a log I have gone over. Since Margaret is not a tall woman and is up to her chest in snow, this log poses a problem. Certain that the Black-backed is by now sated and about to fly off, we desperately beat our way around the log and even before cresting the hill, Margaret cries, "I see it!" Fortunately it is high enough up the tree that she can see it without plowing up the last steep ten metres.

We all get back to the road alive. Success is sweet.

But still no Spruce Grouse or American Three-toed Woodpecker. Nobody else has seen this rare woodpecker and only Jim

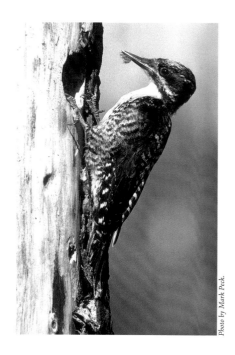

American Three-toed Woodpecker (male). Churchill, Manitoba. In the Algonquin area, this quiet, uncommon bird is usually very hard to find.

Photo by Mark Peck.

Fairchild has seen one Spruce Grouse. Late in the day we search the spruce bog where Jim saw the grouse, but no luck. Margaret patrols the road and Hugh and I plow around in the bog. When I come out of the bog, I see Hugh talking to Margaret and every once in a while taking little stamping ten-metre runs, pounding his feet like a young goat trying out new hooves. *What now?* I wonder. In our last half hour this troubling behaviour only increases, until we get into the car and head back to Whitney for supper.

As we eat, Margaret comments on how fortunate it is that we all stayed so warm even at minus thirty. Hugh allows as to how his feet got "a bit cold near the end," but otherwise he is fine. Now, you should know that Hugh birds almost exclusively in tennis shoes year round since his feet get sore otherwise. In the winter, he occasionally puts on loose-fitting open galoshes over the tennis shoes.

"I wonder how he keeps the snow out of his boots." Margaret says.

"Beats me," I reply.

Looking forward to an early night, we retire to our rooms. I just get my head on the pillow when the TV suddenly blares and Brother Currie commences some prolonged channel surfing, until finally lighting upon a film, which he says should be really good.

"Watch whatever you like," I say. "Nothing will keep me awake."

How wrong I am. *Night of the Killer Mutants* does just that. The death screams and hideous torturing keep on for so long I actually begin to watch myself. Hugh seems to be enjoying it immensely. It's so bad, it's actually interesting.

"It can't go on much longer," I remark after what seems like hours. "Nearly everybody's dead."

"The baby's still gotta get it," says Hugh. He knows these things. We still talk about it.

The next morning Hugh's feet are still cold. I tell him to put on more socks. He does. As we are leaving, he says his feet are *still* cold. And seem wet, if he is not mistaken.

"This won't do," I say. "You're going to put on my extra slush-eaters with the felt liners and two pairs of dry wool socks. Take your galoshes off."

He wants to get going but grudgingly agrees. As he pulls off the first galosh, a great cascade of water comes rushing out. The boot was full of snow all night. Half of the water has already been absorbed by his tennis shoe and socks, but the rest pours out merrily.

Knowing Margaret will never believe this, I take the other boot out to the car and pour the water out of it in front of her. We exchange meaningful looks.

Ten minutes later, with Hugh in warm dry slush-eaters and wool socks, we set out to nail the Spruce Grouse and American Three-toed. Everyone else has gone home and we are the only

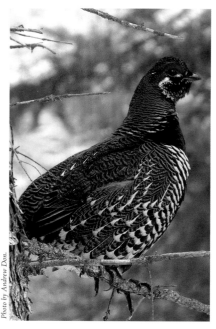

Spruce Grouse (male). Algonquin Provincial Park. True to its nickname, this "fool hen" just sat and gawked in one of its beloved spruce trees.

Photo by Andrew Don.

62

ones searching. No one found a Three-toed Woodpecker on Friday or Saturday. Things look rather grim.

The bird god, however, is with us. At the Spruce Bog Trail, where yesterday there was nothing, we almost immediately get both species. True, Margaret has a bad moment with the woodpecker because her binoculars can't focus under three metres and the bird is almost on top of her, but we cope even with this.

It is hard not to gloat on the way home. We are the only ones to get Common Redpoll and Three-toed Woodpecker and we get all our target species. This does not happen very often. You have to gloat when you get the chance. Believe me.

6

To the Barricades

Once more unto the breach, dear friends, once more.
— SHAKESPEARE, *HENRY IV*, ACT III

BUOYED BY MY SUCCESS IN Algonquin, I move to the attack.
One can't just sit around and wait for May. Anything good
comes up, I'm going to chase it.

A Barrow's Goldeneye turns up again at Presqu'ile Provincial Park and Hugh and I are instantly in hot pursuit. Should
be a piece of cake. Fred Helleiner keeps seeing it out his back
window. The bird is becoming tiresome.

Once, twice, thrice the bird eludes us. On the third trip we view every goldeneye in the Park, except for fifty that fly just before dark as we check our last likely spot. Hugh is sure the Barrow's is among them. He lapses into bitterness and despondency and ponders both giving up birding and death; he says we seem to be the kiss of death. Otherwise he is fine.

The next day, January 30, I return alone and scour the park again. After several hours of fruitless searching, I spy a small flock of goldeneye through the trees on the way to the lighthouse. It will mean traipsing through the snow with improper footwear, but what the hell. Just before staggering out onto the shore, I take a quick peek through the bins in case they flush, and the first bird I see is the Barrow's. Satisfaction is a weak and inadequate word for the feeling one gets at such moments. I am cold and my feet are frozen, but I have found the Grail!

On the way home I decide not to vouchsafe this information to Hugh at this particular time. I'll wait until the despair lifts, you know.

Margaret phones on the evening of February 17. She has just seen a Greater White-fronted Goose and gives precise directions. It's a no-miss situation. Early the next morning I race to the "roadside field simply full of geese" and see a barren expanse of corn stubble, albeit with a creditable quantity of droppings that appear to be on the fresh side. One misshapen European Starling forages briefly in the back corner and then vacates, doubtless having realized that the kiss of death has arrived.

Don't just stand there staring, Stupid, I tell myself. *Think, Poper, think. You can do this. It's not your long suit, but think.*

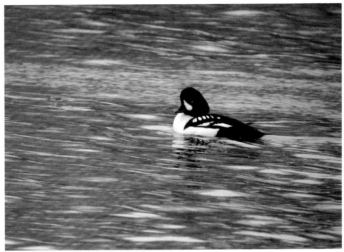

Photo by Jean Iron.

Barrow's Goldeneye (male). Ottawa. Foreheads do not come steeper.

Think like a bird. Where might the geese be now? Hmmm … in the water? Lake Ontario is only one field away. After a good early-morning nosh, they're probably resting on the water.

I hare off down the nearest road to the lake, climb a huge end-of-the-road snow mountain, and see a bay full of geese, one of which looks suspiciously good. I rush back and get my scope. Back up the snowbank, and just as I get on the goose, I realize I am experiencing my first stroke; everything tilts sideways just as I have read. In full knowledge that loss of consciousness, speech, and all feeling in my body will ensue quickly, I try desperately to get a decent look before the inevitable happens. I discover that, by the grace of God, one of my scope legs has sunk deeply into the snowbank, wildly skewing my scope. The stroke narrowly averted, I get right back on the goose. Greater White-fronted! Awright! Nearly cost me my life, but my luck seems to have turned and I feel great. I return to the car singing happily to myself, "Make me feel real loose like a long-necked goose. Like a-oh baby, that's a-what I like." Long live the memory of The Big Bopper. Yeah, Baby.

On February 25 I come close to missing Snowy Owl for the year on Amherst Island. Margaret and I and the Falls clan have seen Short-eared, Long-eared, and Northern Saw-whet Owls but can't find a Snowy anywhere. We have lunch on the roadside in the car. Bruce Falls and Margaret are deep in discussion of the median wing-coverts of juvenile Mackinder's Eagle Owl when a car pulls up behind us and starts flashing its lights desperately. It's Bruce's son, wife, and daughter-in-law; they appear to be pointing up in the air. Tearing myself away with difficulty from the fascinating median covert conversation, I step out and look up. There is a beautiful female Snowy Owl on the telephone pole directly above our car. Let us not ponder how we could have failed to notice it. I don't see another one all year, so this is a biggie. Not Mackinder's Eagle Owl, but a good one nonetheless.

A Harris's Sparrow turns up in Prince Edward County; Margaret and I are off on February 27. As we scream up to the Foxes' feeders (Margaret is driving, of course), we meet two well-satisfied birder-photographers who have just had the bird for over thirty minutes at point-blank range and finally tired of taking pictures. True, it has just flown off — the story of my life — but it is around and coming to the feeder today.

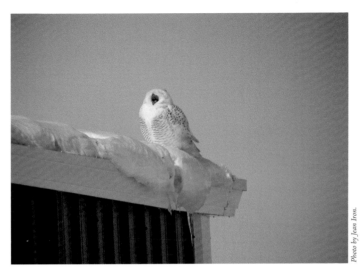

Photo by Jean Iron.

Snowy Owl. Holland Marsh. This is a sight that a vole hopes never to see.

Margaret and I take up position and wait an hour; lots of riff-raff, but no Harris's. Finally, a new flock of sparrows arrives out of nowhere and I think I see the Harris's among them. Confirmation is rendered impossible by the vicious dive-bombing attack of the biggest bloody female Cooper's Hawk I've ever seen. For the next ten minutes we observe a few blowing feathers. Is it to be the Ross's Gull at Port Weller all over again, or has our bird survived? Over the next half hour the flock slowly returns. No Harris's. I am getting hungry and feeling weak, but Margaret is showing no signs at all of losing focus; she stares relentlessly at the feeder. I am ashamed to mention my dreadful leg cramps.

But patience is rewarded — something that rarely happens in real life — and the Harris's suddenly materializes, stays for about fifteen seconds, and then disappears like a ghost, to be seen no more. But I don't care; the fifteen seconds were sweet, even if the bird was in winter plumage and a tad ratty. As Hugh would say, it's a tick.

The next day finally yields a Wild Turkey. I feared for a while to be the only birder in Ontario to miss Wild Turkey in 2007. I'd never *looked* for one before; it was always one of those birds you see all the time when not looking. I also nearly miss the Cobourg Laughing Gull. On March 5, I scan the harbour for hours in the bitter cold and wind before finally attempting to get out of the car and have a further look. I say attempt because I nearly step on the Laughing Gull, which is lounging in the parking lot right beneath my vehicle door waiting for a handout. It is miffed and I have to close my door again quickly. Unlike Doug McRae, I don't routinely stock up on donuts before going for gulls — but then I don't go for gulls in my pyjamas either. As Ron Pittaway later says of this bird, "It was too easy." Not much satisfaction, true — but a tick.

March 12, Gray Partridge seen with Hugh and Andrew Don (Andrew really thinks he spotted them first) right out in the open by the runway at the Brantford airport after a thorough search of the entire surrounding neighbourhood, tramping around in deep snow and grass, Hugh in his tennis shoes.

March 14, I find my own Harlequin Duck at Lucas Point east of Cobourg. A first-winter bird — sweet bird of youth.

March 26, American Woodcock and a close brush with death. I visit Margaret's favourite woodcock site alone at dusk. I look and listen and see diddly-squat. I decide to stray down the road from the car. When it is nearly dark I hear a loud *peent* almost in my ear. I know the bird is very close. Seconds later I see it in all its glory, though to the naked eye it is just a black shape. Let's hear it for the light-gathering power of binoculars. I enjoy the spectacle and flights for ten minutes, until suddenly all hell breaks loose right behind me in the woods. The coyotes go crazy. I can hear their teeth snapping and the drool hitting the ground. Am I the source of such frenzied excitement? I walk briskly, trying hard to give the appearance of nonchalance as I make a beeline for my distant car. How could I have walked so far from it at night? *Stay calm, Poper, stay calm. Do not give in to those powerful, if subliminal, promptings toward lycanthropic delights put forth so urgently in your dreams.* I do not take off my clothes. Before they can swarm me and drink deeply of hot blood, I dive into my car. I open the window and howl madly in frenzied relief.

The next day Margaret says, "Oh, yes, I forgot to mention there is the odd coyote in the area." Yeah, the odd one and a hundred even ones, too. No one ever said birding was safe, though some elderly dotards may actually think so.

April 2, Margaret and I get the Eared Grebe at the Grimsby lagoons. Easy peasy. It comes, however, like most good birds, with a price tag. But I learn a lesson. Instead of taking the easy roundabout way, we decide to head directly for Long Point through the countryside. I have a fairly good

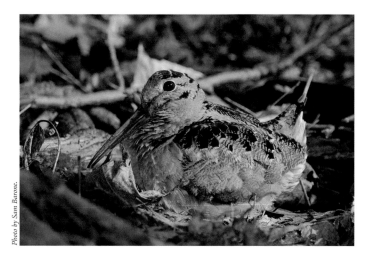

Photo by Sam Barone.

American Woodcock. Rondeau Provincial Park. It can be very difficult to see these birds when they are hunkered down.

idea of how to do it, but since Margaret will be navigating, I relax utterly and bask in the Eared Grebe. We fall to chatting. I mention David Mitchell's stunning tour de force *Cloud Atlas*. Margaret has read the book and has impassioned views. We are about in mid-book when I come to a stop at an unfamiliar T junction. I ask my navigator which way to turn. She hems and haws. None of the many toponyms on the signposts for either direction are familiar. No problem. Margaret will consult the map book. Several minutes of concerned silence, interspersed with uneasy looks at the signposts and the road numbers.

"Odd," says Margaret. "I can't find any of these roads."

There turns out to be a reason for this. Our exact location is three full maps away from where Margaret thinks we are. We have gone hundreds of kilometres out of our way and have to make a huge loop back to get on track. Margaret "can't understand" how it could have happened. I understand exactly. I tell her about the time I was driving from New York to Indianapolis on automatic pilot and apparently took the wrong Y somewhere and ended up at Cleveland before realizing what had happened, thereby adding a full day onto my journey. She is not mollified.

Though we miss the Eurasian Wigeon at Long Point, we do get six new birds and this assuages the grief, pain, humiliation, and mortification, if not the sorrow and despair. I now check maps before having Margaret navigate. And I never discuss literature with her in a moving vehicle.

April 27, I get the Yellow-throated Warbler at Stoney Creek. Quick and easy the way Hughie likes 'em. Fabulous viewing, though Dave Beadle complains plaintively that the bird is too far away for good shots with his video camera, until Andrew Don pishes the bird in so close that Beadle is forced to complain equally bitterly that now the bird is too close. We are all pleased, even Dave, because it is a yellow-lored bird, not the usual *albilora*. Hugh does not mention the grave once on the way home.

May 1, I get the first of many Marbled Godwits for the year on Amherst Island, having been told by a guy without a scope that the bird is definitely not there — a pleasing way to find a bird. I do not know at the time that I shall see many of

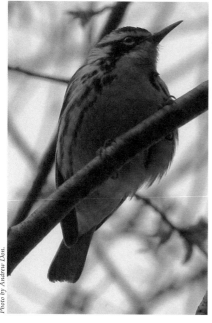

Yellow-throated Warbler. Edgelake Park, Stoney Creek. Andrew pished this rarity down almost into our hands.

Photo by Andrew Don.

these birds all over the province this year. It's good to have a few extras in the bank for the horse-trading on New Year's Eve if one is stuck around 299. You know the kind of thing: I'll give ya three Marbled Godwits, a White Pelican, and as many Black-billed Magpies as you want for your Razorbill or Dickcissel.

All in all, I feel I am in pretty good shape at 182 species before I leave for Point Pelee on May 7.

7

Pelee Madness

God's colors are all fast.

— JOHN GREENLEAF WHITTIER

MONDAY MORNING, MAY 7, FINDS Felicity and me heading for Point Pelee, a riotous kaleidoscope of colours swirling in my mind. We go during the week, since Felicity doesn't enjoy the crush on the Point. Then we spend a week on the Island with peace and quiet where we can visit the Pelee Island Bird Observatory and see warblers in the hand and hear Graeme Gibson the Younger explain the meaning of banding to the birds he so loves (if you have to be banded, this is the guy to be banded by) — and all this for free. Anyway, since we are not going to the annual convention of the North American Phragmites Society, we do not go straight to Stoney Point, in spite of wondrous memories of Yellow-headed Blackbird and Least Bittern in the pre-Phragmites era. This pleases Felicity because it also means we do not have to stop in Comber. She hates Comber; I suppose not least because we never see anything there. She was not there the time in the late fifties when my father and I had the male Kentucky Warbler only three metres away from us foraging in a half-submerged toilet bowl with fetching blue glyphs right beside the lagoon trail. She has no memories of the place. Anyway, she is pleased that for once we are heading for Rondeau Provincial Park to make a quick stop en route to Pelee for a reported Cerulean Warbler.

PELEE AREA TRIP HIGHLIGHTS

Cerulean Warbler. Seen at eye level, feeding just above the water in the pond near the old horse stables at Rondeau — a breathtaking male.

Worm-eating Warbler. Also seen at and below eye level at point-blank range almost necessitating a reverse-bins look in Tilden's Woods in Point Pelee National Park — a very bright peach-coloured male.

Summer Tanager. Seen consuming bees at the "bee tree" at the first Y in Tilden's Woods.

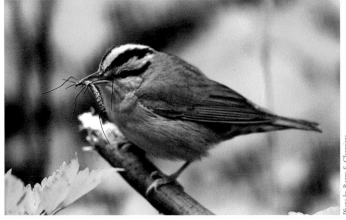

Photo by Barry S. Cherriere.

Worm-eating Warbler. Point Pelee. Difficult to find in Ontario, one does not see this bird every year, even at Pelee.

Henslow's Sparrow. Seen on the trail at the West Beach on the Point. "On the trail" is perhaps not an entirely honest description. The bird has not been spotted for several days and is nowhere to be seen when Hugh and I arrive. I somehow know it is there, back in the grass, and that it will be necessary to go off the trail to find it. So I look long and carefully in all directions, check for hidden surveillance cameras, and wait for the right moment before quickly walking in off the trail, quietly asking Peter Whelan's ghost for forgiveness this one time. Even the legendary Jon Dunn is afraid of the Pelee SS, who can be inappropriately fierce, so it is a risk. But it pays off; I see the bird right in front of me after a short weak flight. You have to get a few of this kind of bird to get to three hundred.

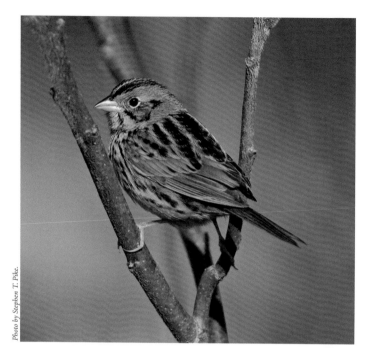

Henslow's Sparrow. West Beach Hiking Trail, Point Pelee. A declining grassland bird, this is a very hard sparrow to find in Ontario.

Yellow-headed Blackbird. Nobody has seen any of these birds but Hugh swears he knows just where they will be on Angler Line on the east side of Lake St. Clair, so we rush up and, sure enough, his favourite marsh has a dozen of them. This leads to an inordinate if brief surge of confidence and wild optimism, which sadly turns out to be totally unwarranted. Things soon go straight downhill.

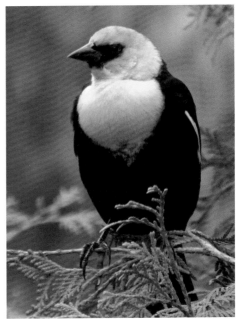

Yellow-headed Blackbird (male). Old Cut, Long Point area. This smashing bird is sadly retreating from most of its haunts in Ontario.

Photo by Jean Iron.

By the time we reach St. Clair Conservation Area, it is teeming rain, and I mean bucketing, but Hugh is riding the wave of optimism and says we are "sure" to get Virginia Rail, Sora, and Least Bittern. He has spent a good deal of time this morning setting up rail and bittern calls on his tapes, and we head off in the rain with Hugh carrying his enormous ghetto blaster, and his friend Diana carrying his large beer-company umbrella and everything else. Our "certainty" of success makes the walk in the driving rain less unpalatable. Hugh plunks down the ghetto blaster at a likely point and says, "Here we go. We'll try for Least

Bittern first." The excitement mounts; my wife is very keen to see this bird. "They should come right in," says Hugh.

Suddenly the air is split with the loudest and most insane cackling imaginable. Somehow the tape has been set for Wild Turkey and the volume is at high. No bitterns respond. No rails come out for a look. In fact, we don't see anything at all for most of our walk. At one point I call a flying Least Bittern, which appears only briefly and then drops out of sight. Everyone else misses it and Hugh becomes very quiet. Black despair sets in. I am glad Felicity and I are in another car. Diana does her best to make light of the incident, to little avail. Ironically I later have to strike Least Bittern from my list because, according to my own rules, I did not get a proper diagnostic look.

Mourning Warbler. Seen on the path while buying a muffin and coffee behind the Visitor Centre. The guy beside me, for whom the bird is a lifer, would have missed it had I not wrested his bins from him and roughly tilted his head downwards. His gratitude knows limits.

Green Heron (Felicity's favourite bird) and **Virginia Rail.** Both in the pond at Fish Point on Pelee Island. Adam Pinch and I are on the viewing platform bewailing the lack of rails when a Virginia Rail strolls out from under the platform and feeds unconcernedly for fifteen minutes.

American Avocet. Three seen at Hillman's Marsh on a quick drop-in on the way back from Pelee Island to Rondeau Provincial Park.

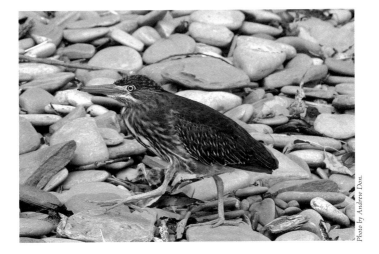

Photo by Andrew Don.

Green Heron (juvenile). Rattray Marsh. The head fluff and streaked neck can still be seen on this young bird.

Yellow-bellied Flycatcher and **Prothonotary Warbler.** Both on the Tulip Tree Trail at Rondeau. The Prothonotary is in his usual slough; the Yellow-bellied is sweet because I find it first by its odd, truncated wood-pewee-type call, which several passing birders insist is just an Eastern Wood-Pewee.

Margaret Atwood. Seen on the north road on Pelee Island carrying laundry to a car. More easily found by searching areas where the garlic mustard has been savagely uprooted — the fresher the uprooting the better. Seventh year in a row. It's a tick.

Fred Bodsworth. This year's Island celebrity birder, and only eighty-eight at this time, seen in a restaurant bar finishing his second beer at 9:00 p.m., surrounded by his exhausted daughters and son-in-law whom Fred has had on the go since about 6:00 a.m. and who can't wait to get to bed. Fred comes over to Felicity and me and asks, "Say, do you guys know any good spots for evening woodcock display?" I do — on the far end of the island. Fred says they will definitely give it a try. I ask him not to reveal to his family who told him about the spot.

MOST CRUSHING DISAPPOINTMENTS

When you go to the Pelee area in May with 182 species under your belt, it is harder to get new birds than it is when your list is more modest and, of course, it gets harder each day to add new species. But you still have to run around like mad trying because you have to get as many of the birds you have counted on seeing as possible while they are all crowded into this one small area and to save having to chase these birds all over the province later. Among my more disappointing misses are: Least Bittern (especially since I think I actually saw one); Sora (I do not even *hear* one at Hillman's); Eastern Screech-Owl; Olive-sided Flycatcher; Acadian Flycatcher; Yellow-throated Vireo; Gray-cheeked Thrush (usually hard to miss); Louisiana Water-thrush; Golden-winged Warbler (I nearly always am lucky with this bird, as Joan Winearls and Barbara Kalthoff can attest, even though it has an obscenely quiet song — quite unforgivable really); Orange-crowned Warbler; Le Conte's Sparrow; Whip-poor-will; Kentucky Warbler; and Yellow-breasted Chat (even at the old cemetery I do not so much as hear one, though both Hugh and Margaret do). Missing Kirtland's Warbler is only a disappointment because on Pelee Island practically everyone I run into has just seen one or more, sometimes many. Somehow Rob Tymstra and I miss all of them, no matter how quickly we check them out. Hmmm.

I at least give the Le Conte's Sparrow a good run for its money. It is reportedly in a grassy field with low shrubs just north of the Park. Hugh and I try for it several times and then enlist the help of some young hotshots, Gavin Platt and Andrew Keaveney, and we go after the bird in earnest. We all get glimpses of an extremely elusive small sparrow, but none of us can identify it for sure. Finally, we see it dart into an isolated clump of shrubs. I say in jest that a *real* birder would go around the field, come up on the shrubs from behind, get down on the ground and do the wiggly-worm through the shrubs, thereby flushing the sparrow out so we could all get a good look. Andrew immediately begins a long, slow lope around the field, comes up to the shrubs, drops onto his stomach, and begins to work his way through like a snake. His girlfriend, who up to this point has perhaps not fully comprehended what she is getting herself into, looks on in consternation. Nothing, of course, flies out. Oh, the bird is there. So, doubtless, are others, but they are all too terrified by this hideous anaconda to fly. But like I said, I gave it my best shot, even if it was Andrew.

May 7 (193). Eleven new birds, including Cerulean Warbler at Rondeau and Black-bellied Plover, Short-billed Dowitcher, and American Pipit at Hillman's Marsh.

May 8 (211). Eighteen new birds, including American Golden-Plover at Hillman's and Red-headed Woodpecker, White-eyed Vireo, Worm-eating Warbler, Northern Waterthrush, Hooded Warbler, Wilson's Warbler, Summer Tanager, Grasshopper Sparrow, Henslow's Sparrow, and Orchard Oriole on the Point.

May 9 (216). Five new birds: Philadelphia Vireo, Prairie Warbler, Canada Warbler, all on the Point; Marsh Wren at St. Clair Wildlife Area; Yellow-headed Blackbird at Angler Line.

May 10 (224). Eight new birds, including Black Tern on the Marsh Boardwalk and Black-billed Cuckoo, Blue-winged Warbler, Tennessee Warbler, and Mourning Warbler on the Point.

May 11 (226). Two new birds: Solitary Sandpiper and Bobolink on Pelee Island.

May 12 (227). One new bird: Blackpoll Warbler on Pelee Island.

May 13 (228). One new bird: Common Moorhen on Pelee Island.

May 14 (230). Two new birds: Green Heron and Virginia Rail on Pelee Island.

May 15 (231). One new bird: Yellow-billed Cuckoo on Pelee Island.

May 16 (235). Four new birds: American Avocet and White-rumped Sandpiper at Hillman's Marsh and Yellow-bellied Flycatcher and Prothonotary Warbler, both on the Tulip Tree Trail at Rondeau Provincial Park.

I return home at 235 with fifty-three new species, including some good ones I might have had a hard time chasing down elsewhere, but I am fifteen short of where I wanted to be and am missing some must-get birds.

Be it duly noted that I am glad, really glad, that my pal John Carley so effortlessly saw the Chuck-will's-widow just after I went home. I am particularly pleased that he had such excellent and prolonged close-up views and derived such immense pleasure from this bird, which would have been a new one for my Ontario life list. Margaret got it, too, — further cause for gladness and joy. She also got Olive-sided and Acadian Flycatcher, Louisiana Waterthrush, Golden-winged and Orange-crowned Warbler, and Yellow-breasted Chat. Boy, am I glad she is not in any way even *trying* to keep ahead of me, let alone competing with me.

All my hopes are now on Rainy River, especially since, for the first time in ages, Thickson's Woods has failed to produce any rarities or southern overshoots this spring. Sadly, Margaret's hip cannot take the long car trip to Rainy River. Nor can Jim Fairchild's health permit, though I do ask him despite the fact that he did sneak up to Parry Sound and get the Blue Grosbeak after we had both decided it was probably too long a shot to merit trying. Hughie and I shall have to try not to pull too far ahead of them.

Heh-heh.

8

The Numbers Build

The Lord giveth …

— AFTER JOB 1:21

BETWEEN MY RETURN FROM PELEE on May 16 and my departure for Rainy River on June 15, I see twenty more species without killing myself (a fact I come to regret later), bringing my total to 255.

Brant (May 23). Jim Fairchild phones and swears there is a Brant floating in the third pond at Nonquon Sewage Lagoons; I am not fussy and go there, alone. My wife says she is busy despite happy memories of our first date. There are people who hold that there is something humorous about sewage lagoons, something to snigger about. Let it be said here and now, I do not number among them. I love a good sewage pond.

All is as Jim said. I feel sorry for the Brant. But it's a tick. I also get my first **Semipalmated Sandpiper** of the year.

Sedge Wren (May 19). Presqu'ile. Margaret hears a tiny chip in the bushes by the beach. I must have been distracted. I didn't hear zip.

"Isn't that a Sedge Wren call note?" she asks modestly.

"Yeah, I think so," I reply. I mean, what are you going to say: "I didn't hear nothin'?" It is, of course, a Sedge Wren, though I believe it has a strangulated syrinx or a hernia and has to call abnormally quietly. I don't feel so bad when Fred Helleiner practically steps on it later. He says, "I didn't realize it was so close."

"What?" I say. "Didn't you hear it chip?"

Whimbrel (May 24). Colonel Sam Smith Park. After failing spectacularly all along the eastern lakefront, I see repeated flocks, plus **Willow Flycatcher** and, finally, **Gray-cheeked Thrush**, which was threatening to become a nemesis bird. I never saw one at Thickson's Woods or Pelee this year.

This is a good day, though not without its dangers. Hugh asked if it was okay if he brought his butterfly net. I unthinkingly said yes. While quietly looking at some interesting sparrow in deep grass, I feel a cold whoosh of air just as my hat is knocked off. Hughie practically decapitates me. "It was an interesting skipper," he says insouciantly, adding sadly, "I missed him."

"Well, you didn't miss me," I say. He seems surprised and mentions something about my not being in the way next time. This experience stands me in good stead the rest of the year whenever I see the ol' net come out. I have fond memories of the *Reisefuehrer* tripping through long-grass meadows in his Bermuda shorts, baseball cap, and ever-present sneakers, pursuing butterflies or dragonflies and looking for all the world like a slightly more manic Nabokov.

Loggerhead Shrike (May 25). Carden Alvar, Wylie Road, out behind bluebird box 10; where else?

Upland Sandpiper (May 25). Wylie Road, teetering on a fence post like a snipe; plus **Vesper Sparrow**, plus **Common Nighthawk** at Alvar Road.

Clay-colored Sparrow (May 26). Cameron Ranch. Turns out I can hear these suckers from seven metres away. Piece of cake. Nothing like the ol' Grasshopper Sparrow, which I practically have to be right on top of. Also **Merlin** in Kirkfield.

Yellow-throated Vireo (May 29). Opinicon Road. Margaret hears it and I locate it in a far-off treetop. I claim to have heard it to save face.

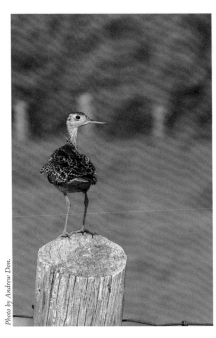

Photo by Andrew Don.

Upland Sandpiper. Carden Alvar. On the alvar, these birds compete for the fence posts with the Wilson's Snipe.

Golden-winged Warbler (May 29). Opinicon Road. Margaret hears it as we drive by talking with the windows closed and the radio on. "Oh, wasn't that a Golden-winged?" asks Margaret unexpectedly. I don't tell her I couldn't hear a Golden-winged if it was perched on my ear and thrust its beak down my ear hole. We jump out and find a little group of them in nearby trees. My faith in Margaret, already considerable, grows. "Well, I'm sure you can at least hear that," says Margaret as they sing away merrily. I claim to be revelling in the concert. I watch carefully. Each time one of them opens his gob, I say, "Oh, wow. Listen to that

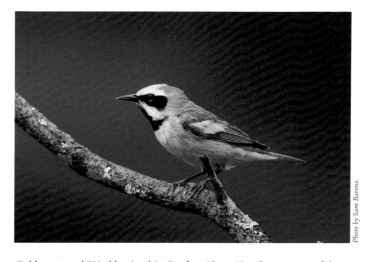

Photo by Sam Barone.

Golden-winged Warbler (male). Carden Alvar. Try showing one of these to a non-birder in your scope!

little guy." This technique works well with Brown Creeper also, I find. Just don't get out of sync.

Alder Flycatcher (Number 250! May 29. It is at this stage that I start my countdown, numbering every bird.). We find the bird east of Cobourg in a special place Margaret knows. The bird drives me crazy with its calling before it finally zips out and sits on the wires for a minute before hiding again.

Ruddy Turnstone (251, June 1). Cobourg Harbour, crawling all over the broken cement slab breakwater; not scenic, but it beats having them stealing fries from your dinner table in Tobago.

Northern Bobwhite (June 4). Long Point area. I think I have a bird for my heard-only extras list. Bruce Falls counted this bird on his Baillie Birdathon and charged everybody for it. I figure if it was good enough for Dr. Falls, it is good enough for me. But I am wrong. I soon find out it is not good enough for the OBRC (Ontario Bird Records Committee). Apparently these birds are considered releases or escapees. Damn. And Bruce won't give me my money back! He tries to claim his wasn't an escapee. This doesn't work when I try to use it on Margaret. The OBRC owes me one.

Cattle Egret (252, June 4). Seen from the car, head deep in cow dung near the poetically named town of Gasline.

Lark Sparrow (253, June 4). Long Point area. Margaret and I nearly miss this bird until Hugh staggers across a lumpy field and flushes it out to the edge. We know from his body language he has either been attacked by killer bees or has seen the bird. We rush to the area toward which he is charging and get the bird in an open tree. I like them. Got a decent song on them, you know. No mealy-mouthing.

Louisiana Waterthrush (254, June 4). Long Point area. This bird calls all around us for half an hour, repeatedly flying unseen from the forest floor to the canopy. Margaret sees it. Hugh sees it. Somehow I don't. We resort to tapes. The bird begins to tear around and I get repeated glimpses of it. I keep playing the tape though I know I shouldn't. I remember my vows, but I can do no other. Finally, I get my diagnostic view of it in a treetop. I ask it what the hell it is doing in a treetop, but it just gawks. This is my one overuse of tapes all year. I feel bad, but not quite as bad as if I had missed the bird. I do not want to have to look for the already much harassed Ganaraska Forest bird closer to home.

Least Bittern (255, June 13). Lone Pine Marsh. After numerous attempts, in clouds of mosquitoes and up to my thighs in duck weed, I get a close up fly-by of a breeding pair, the female followed seconds later by the male, after which the flies seem a good deal less troublesome.

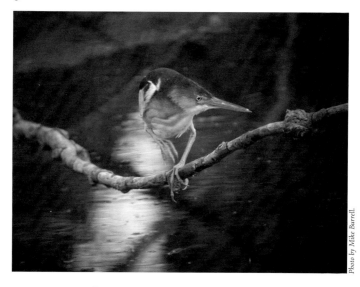

Photo by Mike Burrell.

Least Bittern. Hillman's Marsh. This cooperative bird forgot how notoriously hard to find it is supposed to be.

A number of these birds (Yellow-throated Vireo, Golden-winged Warbler, Louisiana Waterthrush, Least Bittern) were birds I hoped to get at Pelee and then had to make time to chase and find elsewhere later, when I could have been after other birds. See everything you can at Pelee or pay the price later.

9

Rainy River

And the Lord taketh away.

— AFTER JOB 1:21

HUGH HAS SEVERAL YOUNG HOTSHOTS with keen ears lined up to accompany us to Rainy River but they drop away one by one, thereby missing the opportunity of a lifetime to bird with Hugh and me. Hugh is determined not to be stuck with me alone, a great confidence builder, and begins to ask around. Bob Carswell jumps at the opportunity, figuring he'll get a few laughs if nothing else. He will get more than he bargained for. He's got better ears than we do and he drinks, so I figure we haven't done too badly.

Friday June 15 finds us heading north in a stately PT Cruiser, which Hugh has managed to rent on an unlimited mileage basis. When the woman asked our destination, just as I was about to say Rainy River, Hugh said, "Oh, we're heading up Sudbury way and maybe a bit west of there." I was not there when he returned it with five thousand kilometres on it. They can't have been too angry, however, because they gave him free baseball tickets, which thrilled him.

As we cruise north, we are in high spirits. I should be able to make up for any losses at Pelee. I hope to get twenty new species, which would put me at 275 in late June, a pretty good gaming position with over six months to get the remaining twenty-five birds and then some. Coady would be getting nervous if only he knew.

We talk of possible birds. Connecticut Warbler, which I did not bother to chase even when I was at Colonel Sam's when one was being seen — it was only a female, for heaven's sake — is a sure thing. In the bag, so to speak. Jean Iron assured me they would be dripping off the trees at eye level at close range. I consider adding it to my list even before leaving, but decide it will be more fun to wait until I actually see my first one for the trip. And, of course, Yellow Rail is another no-miss bird at Rainy River. Glenn Coady says there were kazillions of them last time he was at Rainy River and all the books list them in numerous places. But why waste time; just go to Fred's Marsh, knock the bird off, and get on with things.

We talk of other slightly less certain birds: Western Kingbird, Sprague's Pipit, Western Tanager, Western Grebe, Mountain

Bluebird, and even Western Wood-Pewee. All seem likely at Barrie, possible at Sudbury, and highly unlikely at Sault Ste. Marie. Somehow they become progressively less likely as we near our destination. Why does this invariably happen? "Probably won't get any of them," says Hugh morosely; not half as morosely, of course, as on our way home when we have indeed failed to see any of the aforementioned.

But my spirits remain high. Hugh tells us three or four hundred of his favourite limericks. Carswell unknowingly encourages him; even writes a few of the more scabrous ones down. In revenge, I get Hugh onto lawyer jokes of which he has an inexhaustible store and we all have some good laughs, particularly Hugh. Lawyer jokes somehow become a fixture on the trip. True, Bob does not find the wit quite as sharp as Hugh does and does not beg for more, but then Bob is a lawyer and may even have heard some of them. It is a long trip for him.

As expected, I get a new bird even on the first day. Hugh tells us when to start expecting Brewer's Blackbird and several telephone poles later we see our first of many. The area around Desbarats has lots of them. Oh, man. **Brewer's Blackbird** (256)! I'm on a roll already.

My spirits are only slightly dampened by the flirtatious and ultimately dastardly behaviour of a King Rail at Pumpkin Point Marsh before the Sault. This is a fabulous marsh with an excellent viewing platform from which we see many good birds, but no King Rail, though we hear him. Oh, yes, we *hear* him, repeatedly, all around us. We try to sucker him out with tapes, but no deal. He plays coy. He isn't interested in being

seen. After frequent near misses almost right underneath us —
as he keeps changing sides — we give up and I have to relegate
this bird to my heard-only list, where it will remain. Damn!

Things go further downhill at our motel near Wawa. It has
Internet service and we log on to Ontbirds. Indecently quickly,
after my departure from Cobourg, Margaret has posted a
Glossy Ibis in the area. My heart soars with joy for her. I cry
myself to sleep.

Saturday June 16 we have lunch in beautiful Rossport then
motor on to Atikokan, where we stay in the old hotel, a favourite of mine, particularly because of the breakfast — and Hugh
loves the price. My old friend, Dave Elder, comes and has breakfast with us and gets us all revved up. No mega-rarities to report,
but he tells us exactly where to see many of our desiderata. My
only fear is that they will all be like the Cobourg Laughing Gull
— too easy. I like a four-to-five second wait to add a little frisson
of angst to the kill.

By noon on Sunday June 17 we are west of Fort Frances and heading west along the Rainy River Road. I feel good
things are about to happen. They do.

Off to the left over the river we see our first of myriad **American White Pelicans** (257), making my later sighting at Cootes
Paradise in Hamilton somewhat less thrilling. Then we stop to
check a field and I have a **Sharp-tailed Grouse** (258) fly right
by me. Sadly, Hugh and Bob are down the road the other way
and do not get this bird, but we do see others on the ground at
Rainy River. After a quick cry, we press on. **Black-billed Magpie**
(259)! We all see it and then scores of others. Ditto for **Western**

Meadowlark (260) and **Franklin's Gull** (261). By the time we reach Budreau's Oak Grove Camp, which is to be our base, I have five new birds for the day, which puts me right on schedule. These five plus Brewer's Blackbird mean I only have to see fourteen more in three and a half days, not counting the trip home.

On Monday June 18, I only see one new bird; at least it's a good one — **Piping Plover** (262). We hear from Dan Lee, who is also staying at Budreau's, that there is a nest on a sand island off Windy Point. It has apparently been marked off by the MNR. We hire a boat to take us out and drop us on the point, which is only just possible because of the wind; the name Windy Point does not turn out to be a misnomer. After a brief distraction ogling the many Yellow-headed Blackbirds and Franklin's Gulls, we ascertain that indeed there are no Piping Plovers on the point. However, we do see what looks like a marker on the last of a series of flat, sandy, windswept islands just out of scoping range. Getting there could be dangerous. The wind is howling and the water rough and white-capped. While trying to make up my mind whether or not to go for it, I turn to consult with Hugh and am shocked to see how white his legs look; he already has his pants off. I hope he can swim. Oh, well, he must float (sorry, Hugh). We anchor our clothes and scopes and set off, having both left statements for the police and loved ones with Bob, who is happy to stay on the point. Many of the birds there are new for him this year and he does not *need* Piping Plover the way Hugh and I do.

It is rough going — hard on the feet and hard to lift a foot without being blown over. It is a further trial to be swarmed by hundreds of gorgeous Franklin's Gulls in full breeding plumage in dazzling sunlight and wind as we pass the first sandy islands, but we cope. A surfeit of beauty can be fatal, you know. As we approach the last island, we stop and scan it. Sure enough there is a yellow marker and the nest nearby in the sand. We can see a Piping Plover sitting on the nest, eyeing us closely. We immediately indulge in a round of high-fives. I do not stop to ponder what the plover makes of two semi-naked senior citizens standing up to their knees in water in a typhoon making high-fives, but it is at this point in the trip that Carswell starts locking his door at night. Hugh and I do not go a step closer, especially with all the gulls around. We take a long careful look and turn around. How Brother Currie stays upright is beyond me, but somehow we both make it back.

Monday evening Carswell and Pope briefly assume panic stations. We hear a cry of horror from Hugh's bedroom. We rush to the rescue and find him pointing at a tiny dark reddish spot moving along his arm. "It's a tick," I say. Brother Currie is not amused. I execute the tick and we are able to go to bed, though Hugh imagines ticks crawling on him all night long. This is the first of many ticks attracted to the *Reisefuehrer*, though Bob and I have no problems. I tell Hugh he's a tick magnet. This also does not amuse him. Days after our return, he locates a tick bite with an aureole behind his knee and has to undergo a round of antibiotics. Mosquitoes love him, too.

Tuesday June 19. No new birds. Carswell nearly drowns in Fred's Marsh and we neither hear nor see a single Yellow Rail or Le Conte's Sparrow. The deep water in the fields is all the result of recent rains. The whole area suffered a severe drought in May and the rails have given the area a pass this year. May they roast in hell. They are nowhere to be found. At this stage I'd gladly crush a hundred baby rails with a steel cable just to glimpse one. So much for my fears of attack-Yellow Rails.

I must qualify my statement that we did not see a single Le Conte's Sparrow. While Bob was swimming back to the car, I did flush a small sparrow which flew ahead of me and over toward Hugh and disappeared in a low island of shrubbery. Hugh thought it might have been a Le Conte's, but after careful searching, all we found was a Clay-colored Sparrow at the spot. Hughie fell to brooding and said nothing else.

Wednesday June 20. No new birds. It is a dirty, windy day. Dan Lee generously takes us around to all kinds of little-known spots and the best we can do is hear one Connecticut Warbler — and only just. Dan is amazed because he has been seeing all kinds of them. Are we, then, the kiss of death? If they are dripping off the trees, it is only on the back side of the spruce bogs this year. The bird I didn't chase at Colonel Sam's flies back to haunt me. Only later do I learn that a determined Fred Bodsworth spent several weeks in June trying to see a Connecticut north of Lake Superior in spite of being eighty-eight and having cataracts on both eyes. He had to settle for a small shape speeding low across a road. I didn't feel so bad after hearing that. We weren't the only ones. And at least I have one more for my heard-only list.

Things seem rather grim. We have to take Bob to the Thunder Bay airport by noon on Thursday and I'm stuck at 262. I am a loser. Hugh talks about spending more time on Scrabble and bridge in the future. He wonders what's happening in the obits. Bob speaks of all the wonderful birds we are seeing. He seems to have lost perspective.

Thursday morning, June 21. We have three hours before heading for the airport. We discuss what to do. Hugh says he wants to return to Fred's Marsh. Bob, who has been unable to acquire a wetsuit, is not all that keen, but Hugh insists.

"Why?" I ask.

"Le Conte's Sparrow," says Hugh. "I think that was a Le Conte's we saw on Wednesday."

"But we chased that bird and it was a Clay-colored."

"That was a different bird," says Hugh. "I saw the one you flushed, flying, and I think it was a Le Conte's." It's been keeping him awake at night.

Well, Bob and I realize we'll never hear the end of it if we don't go, and we have no better prospects anyway, and since Bob is happy to bird the surrounding dry area, we head off. Humour the old guy, you know. Poor old Hughie.

I start up the centre of the drowned field, and halfway across, right where I flushed the bird before, I hear a Le Conte's Sparrow. Hugh was right! I know this call and I also know that if I hear it well, the bird is close, damn close. I freeze. The singing goes on. I search desperately. I take down my bins and see the **Le Conte's** (263) seven metres in front of me perched on some bent grass just above water level — probably by a nest. I signal Hugh. He stares at me. He puts up his bins and I mouth "Le Conte's," and point ahead. For a largish man he does zero to sixty rather

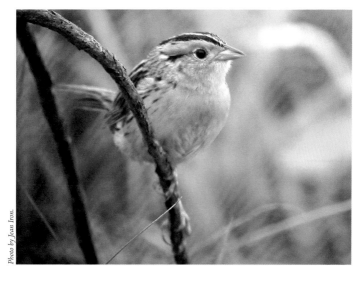

Photo by Jean Iron.

Le Conte's Sparrow. Rainy River. Though hard to find, the beautiful head pattern of these birds makes the search worthwhile.

quickly and comes charging through the paddy, cutting a swath like a startled rhino and leaving a considerable wake behind him. I desperately signal for him to stop as he approaches.

"Where is it?" he asks.

I point right in front of me and he sees it. Victory is ours and it is sweet; sweet enough to hold us all the way to the Thunder Bay airport where we part with Bob. It was a good trip, eh Bob?

Bob made the right move flying home. Hugh and I drive back the long northern route through Nipigon, Geraldton, Hearst, Kapuskasing, Cochrane, and Timmins, and fail to find

Olive-sided Flycatcher in 3,477 perfect bogs, including a desperation last-minute visit to Wolf Howl Pond in Algonquin, where the bird is usually hard to avoid. And Bridget Stutchbury thinks *her* birds are in trouble. Also, no Hawk Owls, Great Gray flybys, or anything else for that matter. Oh, yes, we do *hear* Pine Grosbeak, which gives me a third heard-only bird — big deal.

So, I'm at 263 instead of 275. Rainy River was thin like Thickson's Woods this year; just my luck. Hugh says I probably won't make it now. It's virtually all over. But I secretly still have the bit in my teeth. We'll see.

10

Making It Happen

Hope springs eternal in the human breast.

— ALEXANDER POPE, *AN ESSAY ON MAN*

JULY 1 AND I'M STILL at 263, twelve birds behind my self-imposed schedule, and Hugh says things are looking bad. Okay, I've got to make it happen. I shall not allow myself to suffer ignominy and shameful defeat without a battle. It'll be like an exam in high school; I'll let on I'm not even really trying any more, but go like hell behind the scenes.

Northern Goshawk (264, July 6, Kilbride). These birds have bred on my Haliburton property for years, but do you think they are around this year? Ha! They've disappeared without trace or reason, unless they are in on some kind of conspiracy with the gods — not to be ruled out, the way things are going. Hugh says we should try for the bird seen at Kilbride, where there's supposed to be a nest and the bird is terrorizing local kiddies. Sounds very hopeful. At least it has food and may stick around.

We arrive, park at the described spot, and immediately see an empty nest in a big white pine, but I know it's not a goshawk nest. I head up the road while Hugh roots around in the back of the car with one hand, keeping the other free to ward off the hordes of mosquitoes that have already found him. God knows what he is looking for. I hear a Gos just off the road. I wave madly to Hugh who arrives, running, in full equipment featuring a very substantial bicycle helmet. He looks like an entrant in a roller derby. We head in, for some reason with me in the lead. Just as we spot her — a seemingly huge immature bird — she makes her first pass at us. I expect Hugh to step up to the plate and take the first hit, but he rather cravenly hunkers down behind me. I feel the rush of the wings. She circles.

"Do we need a better look?" I ask. We agree we should vacate quickly, and begin to backtrack. The second pass is less aggressive and not as close. We retreat with a modicum of dignity.

"I brought a helmet for you but couldn't find it," says Hugh. Thanks, pal.

Barred Owl (265, July 16, Straggle Lake, Haliburton). I wonder, is this to be the first time in thirty-five years I have missed Barred Owl on my own property? Finally one flies ahead of me and lands just down the road. I now know I will see Barred Owls constantly all summer, and I do. They no longer need to hide from me.

Eurasian Collared-Dove (266, July 20, Stoney Creek). Hugh and Andrew Don and I scream to a stop on the corner where the bird is supposed to be. Before Andrew is out of the car, I hear the bird and tell Andrew. Andrew assumes I am kidding him but looks up anyway and finds the bird practically on top of us. It is a first in Ontario for Andrew and me. It's the Laughing Gull all over again — too easy — but I'll take it. As Hughie would say, it's a tick.

Acadian Flycatcher (267, July 20, Spooky Hollow). As always, Hugh has "exact" instructions for an active nest, right to the branch. "Take trail X, you can't miss it, go several hundred yards 'or so,' take the first left and then immediately go right, go on for a bit, take two lefts and then a right, proceed for a while and look up, and Bob's your uncle." We never even find the no-miss trail X. We try the instructions on numerous trails, but nothing fits. Hugh "just can't understand it," though my heart sank the minute he read out the instructions. We fan out in despair and try to find our own bird.

Hugh yells, "I just heard one."

Yeah, I think, *you couldn't hear it if it were on your head*. It is an unchristian thought. But to humour him, Andrew and I go over, getting our feet soaked in a boggy patch. Hugh says it hasn't called again. I don't say that I didn't think it would. This is fortunate, because right above us an Acadian Flycatcher suddenly calls and flies out of one leafy maple top into another even more impenetrable one. After a prolonged chase, we all finally get satisfactory looks at the bird. Never underestimate the *Reisefuehrer*. His hearing can be quite good when he wants it to be. Try whispering "doughnuts" or "Tim Hortons" at ten metres in a wind.

Stilt Sandpiper (268, July 20, Jarvis Sewage Lagoons). Andrew and Hugh and I are on a roll. We immediately find a dark breeding-plumaged adult, heavily striped from neck to tail underneath. There are no other birds at the lagoon that I *need*, but three new species in one day is pretty good going. It won't happen often again this year.

Sanderling (269, July 26, Cobourg Harbour). Home sweet home; an easy one.

Baird's Sandpiper (270, August 19, Presqu'ile). No new birds since July 26 — a long, seemingly endless, doldrums period — so this is a welcome bird, the first of a very high number of Baird's Sandpipers I will see this year at Chatterton Point in Presqu'ile Provincial Park.

Red-necked Phalarope (271, August 19, Nonquon Sewage Lagoons). Ron Pittaway posts these birds on Ontbirds and I rush up immediately and score. Yes!

Willet (272, August 19, Cranberry Marsh). Another Ontbirds posting and I get it on my first attempt. I arrive late in the day and, risking imprisonment and possible water boarding, I drive down the road for AUTHORIZED VEHICLES ONLY. I have a story ready if I'm arrested. After finding the bird and successfully sneaking back out, I find that I feel only the slightest guilt. This is not like me. I am usually a law-abiding rabbit who worries himself sick at any minor illegality. I am becoming venal and corrupt.

Olive-sided Flycatcher (273, August 26, Cobourg). This has become my nemesis bird. Remember, Hugh and I drove two thousand kilometres looking for one on the way back from Rainy River with no luck. All summer I stare at appropriate perches and rack up a huge count of Eastern Kingbirds, Cedar Waxwings, and Starlings, but no Olive-sided. We are now into prime time — their migration week. As with many other birds, there is only a short time period within which you have a fairly good chance of seeing this bird not on its breeding grounds. Others are starting to see them. Jean Iron is suffering sleep deprivation because one sings madly outside her window at five in the morning from an unnaturally visible perch. Doug McRae told me in the spring that Olive-sided should be in the dead cottonwoods in the Fingers at Presqu'ile on August 22 or 23. I search the cottonwoods for several days. Not a hint of one when I'm there. McRae probably sees several hundred of them. I don't ask. I am profoundly discouraged.

Hugh steps up to the plate and says we are going to Presqu'ile to find this bird. He comes to my house in Cobourg.

We set off. Two blocks later, at the intersection of King and D'Arcy streets, as I am turning left, I see a bird at the top of a dead branch in a huge white ash. I point it out to Hugh and stop the car.

"Probably my two millionth Cedar Waxwing, but check it out."

"Looks pretty good," says Hugh.

We get out. It looks *very* good. I get my scope out. We have excellent looks and indulge in mad high-fives. Only now do I begin to perceive horns and angry yells as cars swing around my vehicle which is stopped diagonally with the doors open in the middle of the busy intersection in mid-left turn. Some drivers lack both a sense of humour and the milk of human kindness.

I tell Margaret immediately, even though she doesn't *need* Olive-sided. "We have the perfect tree for next year," I tell her. Two days later she calls and tells me they have cut down the big ash. It turns out to be true, even though it was sound as a hound's tooth right through. I guess they didn't want me seeing one two years in a row.

Long-billed Dowitcher (274, August 26, Brighton Wetlands, "Chez Tiny" — please note that this is not a sewage lagoon, certainly not. It is a "water polishing facility.") Hugh and I find this early migrant and have to wait weeks before the others begin to arrive.

Red Knot (275, August 27, Presqu'ile). I meet Maureen Riggs with her husband at the Beach Four parking lot. She is very disappointed to have missed the Whimbrels, about which I, for once, care little.

"Only saw a Red Knot just at the end of the path."

Hoping I remembered to thank her, I tear off like one possessed. Of course, when I arrive the Red Knot is gone and a small group of Whimbrels are serenely feeding. Such is birding. Dejectedly, I trudge on to Owen Point and the gods decide to humour me. I find the Red Knot in gray fall plumage; a far cry from its spring splendour, but it's a Red Knot just the same and still a very nice bird. I am pleased. You can't have everything. I have not become like Joan Winearls, who only really countenances male warblers in full breeding colours. I have not sunk that far. Oh, all right, possibly with hummingbirds.

Buff-breasted Sandpiper (276, September 8, Beeton Sod Farms — you have to be careful and explain to English people what a sod farm is. It can raise eyebrows.) After much chasing around and enriching various oil sheiks, Hugh and I finally find these birds just as a Merlin nails a hapless Killdeer beside them and flies off to consume it nearby. I have a crummy look at the panicked Buff-breasteds, and every shorebird within miles flies high into the air and heads south. Do I count them or not? I shouldn't, but … Later we find them again and have long, satisfying looks. I return home triumphant and call Margaret.

"Oh," she says, "Buff-breasted. They've been all over our harbour today."

I am glad she has had such good looks and gotten them so effortlessly. Glad. Yes, glad.

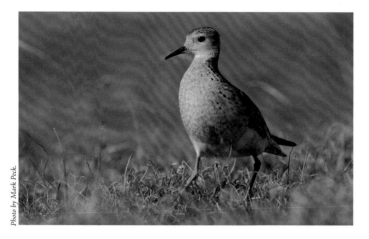

Photo by Mark Peck.

Buff-breasted Sandpiper. Cambridge Bay, Nunavut. These birds touch down in Southern Ontario only briefly during the fall migration.

Sabine's Gull (277, September 8, Van Wagner's Beach). I am disappointed today to have to settle for one unidentified jaeger — I'm not going the "jaeger sp." route (which allows you to count one jaeger species until you definitely identify one later), unless I'm at 299 on New Year's Eve. But just before leaving, Barry Cherriere yells, "Sabine's Gull." I suddenly know I'm going to miss this bird. I can't find it as Barry methodically describes its flight path. Worse still, Hugh finds it easily and immediately. He eventually puts it in my scope for me. Oh, well, at least I see it and have a good look.

Eastern Screech-Owl (278, September 18, Cobourg). Nobody can believe I haven't seen one yet. Even I can't believe it, and I've

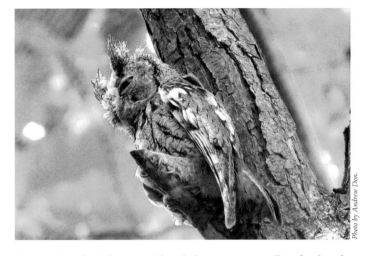

Photo by Andrew Don.

Eastern Screech-Owl. Bronte. Though their quavering call is often heard, these nocturnal birds are seldom seen.

looked for them. None of this waiting until I stumble on one. Remember, I'm trying to make things happen these days. Margaret gets tired of this and decides to take me to her secret spot *di tutti* spots where it is impossible to miss screech-owls. She calls her friend first; they are everywhere. What colour do you want? So we go, and … nada. Not even a response. It is a dreadful humiliation for Margaret's screech-owl guru, to say nothing of Margaret herself. We go on to a spot Doug McRae has told me about and get all kinds of responses to our tape (it goes on my heard-only list), but no owl manifests itself, even in a flyby.

Margaret calls several days later. Bruce Parker has one in his backyard that reliably comes in to a tape. Reliably? Yeah, sure. I'm over there that evening, trying not to look needy. I don't want Parker to think I'm a complete rookie. Nor do I wish him to be humiliated. He doesn't know there is some kind of conspiracy afoot. Bruce takes me out back, plays one call, and I'm practically bombed by a gray-morph owl that comes right in and sits above me, gawking. Parker takes it in his stride and I try not to look too thrilled. Eastern Screech-Owl comes off my heard-only list.

11

Revelations

Whenever a friend succeeds, a little something in me dies.
It is not enough to succeed. Others must fail.

— GORE VIDAL

I AM NOT A VERY nice person. Oddly, before my Big Year, even while pursuing it at the beginning, I had thought I was a nice fellow, full of the milk of human kindness. But now I know the bitter truth. I am a malicious and spiteful person, an ingrate, a scoundrel — in short, a knave. Yes, a knave.

When Margaret and I are tied at 279 in mid-September, I call to tell her I will be away for several days in Stratford with my wife.

Silence. Then a small voice. "You won't have time to try for the Ruff at Harrington, will you?"

"The Ruff? Oh, probably not," I reply, not entirely truthfully, as I already have my scope in the car and a printout of the exact location near Stratford. "Oh, I might give it a try if I can find the time, but we'll be pretty busy what with seeing two plays and everything."

The next afternoon, September 19, Felicity and I, as planned, drive straight to Harrington and I knock off the **Ruff** (279). Yes! But I can't help feeling guilty. "Margaret's not gonna like this," I say out loud.

"Nonsense. She'll be thrilled for you," says Felicity innocently.

Some sixth sense nags at me, however, suggesting otherwise. This is decidedly uncharitable of me and I finally take myself to task. Margaret is a very generous person. Of course she'll be thrilled.

The next evening I call Margaret. "Hi, Margaret. I'm back from Stratford. The plays were awesome. You must try to see Graham Greene as Lennie in *Of Mice and Men*. He was brilliant."

"Did you see the Ruff?" asks Margaret, never one to beat around the bush.

"The Ruff? Ah, yeah, actually I did."

"Oh, I *knew* you would," says Margaret bitterly. Then recovering herself, she adds, "I'm very glad," like we aren't in competition or anything.

"I didn't get that good a look at it," I say weakly, trying to put a better face on things. "Just a juv, you know."

"I'm glad for you," repeats Margaret icily.

Oh, dear, I think. *What have I done?*

Fortunately the whole issue blows over in several days because Margaret has to go to Toronto to perform grandmotherly babysitting duties, and while there she "slipped over to Harrington and got the Ruff." (I don't like to ask how long the children were alone and under what circumstances.)

I am genuinely happy for her until I realize she has pulled even again and might even pull ahead of me.

And that "Oh, I *knew* you would" nags at me. Margaret was not full of sudden pure childlike joy when her old birding buddy got his Ruff. Yet Margaret is my friend. Friends revel in each other's success, don't they? I ponder this mystery for the better part of a month.

On October 22, when Margaret and I are tied at 290, I am working at home quite at peace with myself. There is nothing that has to be chased, and I can finally start getting caught up on some of my household duties in which I have been signally derelict. And I know for a fact that Margaret is so far behind in her work that she is perforce devoting all this day *and* the next two to clearing her desk, and there can sadly be no question of chasing any bird, no matter how good. I know this because she herself has told me so, categorically. Anything good shows up, I'll be on my own.

At 2:55 in the afternoon I notice the grass in our backyard is almost waist high. Didn't Felicity say something about my cutting the lawn if it weren't an imposition on my valuable birding time? I believe she did. I will surprise her. I tackle the lawn.

When I am about halfway done, I remember that I am supposed to take the lamb out of the freezer to thaw.

I rush inside and take out the chops, and only as I turn to go back out do I notice the red message light on the phone flashing.

I pick up the phone. "Oh, hello. It's Margaret. It's, ah, three o'clock. I presume you have already left for the Ross's Goose at Reesor Pond that Stan Long has just posted. I thought we could go together [a note of bitterness?]. Perhaps I'll see you there. Hold it for me."

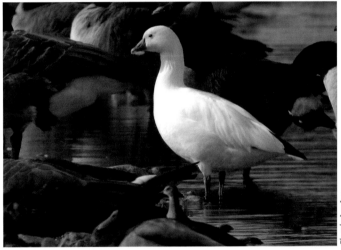

Photo by Jean Iron.

Ross's Goose. Reesor Pond. This attractive little goose is a welcome visitor in Ontario in the spring and fall migrations.

Oh, my God. My thrice-accursed computer has been down and I have not been able to check my email. Margaret tried to alert me. I look at my watch. Four forty-five. I could perhaps just get there in time, but would have to fight the traffic all the way back to Cobourg, miss supper, leave the lawn half-mown, and spoil Felicity's evening.

I agonize. What to do? What would Coady do in such a situation? I ponder this for several seconds, but the answer is clear. Then I think of all the consequences and decide not to go. I'm not even a real twitcher. I am bogus.

I go back outside and begin fitfully mowing again. *Two-ninety-one for Margaret* keeps going through my head. I knew she'd pull ahead. And there's no way that bird will hang around until morning. But I'll still have to head out at 5:00 a.m. to be there for first light to maybe see a few white feathers where it will have taken off. I should have gone today. Any real birder would be on the 401 at 130 kilometres per hour right now. What a loser. Bet it's a nice adult, too.

Margaret will be pleased. I try to tell myself how glad I am for her, but my joy seems oddly limited and even disingenuous. Yet, I must be pleased for her. I am her friend.

At 6:00 p.m. the phone rings. I look at the call display. It's Margaret calling to gloat. I can't pick up the phone. Felicity picks it up.

"Hello, Margaret. What?" Pause. "Oh, dear. Oh, how disappointing. Yes, he's right here. I'll give him to you."

There is a god. Margaret has dipped on the goose. My heart soars up like a skylark uncontained.

"Hi, Margaret. Did you get the goose? Oh, no! Oh, I'm so sorry. Bummer, eh? No sign of it? Oh, dear, what a disappointment. And all that driving for nothing! Yes, I know how busy you were. This'll really set you back."

Heh-heh.

We're still even. I haven't missed anything and I don't have to get up with the hens tomorrow. I can relax and have a little glass of something red with my supper. Live a bit.

Everything has worked out for the best.

Only something is bothering me. What could it be? Deep down I know. It's because I'm glad Margaret did not get the goose. I didn't really want her to be disappointed, but I am pleased, well pleased, that she didn't get the goose.

Whence all my *schadenfreude* (the malicious enjoyment of another's misfortune)? And what kind of a person would experience such feelings for a friend's misfortune?

The answer comes through with great clarity: not a very nice person — in short, a scumbag. What a time to discover that I am a knave. I'm sixty-bloody-five! I'd always pictured myself like the kindly, grandfatherly Lenin, smiling at the young cherubs gathered round his feet in my favourite Socialist Realist painting. Then, suddenly, you discover your imagined persona is a fiction and your real one has near Hitlerian proportions. Hitler didn't love the competition either, you know.

I'm just beginning to enjoy retirement and I have to make this discovery. Oh, eschew the *annus mirabilis*, my friends. Eschew it like the plague. It brings with it unsought revelations and self-knowledge troubling to the carefree soul.

I take myself severely to task. I have my dark night of the soul. Compared to my lowliness, Margaret's "Oh, I *knew* you would" is a piddling venial sin. I resolve to never again allow myself to rejoice in Margaret's or *any* friend's failures, especially

Hugh's. Away *schadenfreude*, unworthy temptation. Hello true compassion. From now on I shall be a better person, kinder and more understanding, quick to help others and revel in their successes. I shall bathe Carley in brotherly love and stress how wonderful it is that he got the Chuck-will's-widow. I shall begin to kiss my rivals' cheeks. Let them think what they will. I was blind, but now I see!

Only, dear God, just don't test me on a Wheatear or Field-fare or something.

12

The Big Sit

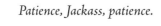

Patience, Jackass, patience.

— Dame Edith Sitwell to Chairman Mao

My wife and I had a good laugh on Pelee Island back in May.

I came back from Fish Point around 8:00 a.m. for breakfast on our back porch, from which you can see the whole point. We stay in the southernmost building in Canada. I put my scope on the end of the point and asked her to have a look.

"There's some madman sitting out there all by himself," she said.

"Oh, did I not mention it? It's Tymstra," I replied, referring to our birding friend and island stalwart, Rob Tymstra. "He's doing a Big Sit."

"A what?" asked Felicity.

"A Big Sit," I explained, as if there was nothing the slightest bit odd about it. "You choose some place and go sit there for the whole day and record all the birds you see."

"Don't you get hungry?"

"You take food with you and chairs and stuff, though I must say Rob didn't seem to have too much food with him. He said something about people bringing him coffee and doughnuts from Tim Hortons."

"But there is no Tim Hortons on the island, or any dough- nut shop for that matter."

She had a point.

When we checked Fish Point later that afternoon, there was no sign of Tymstra. He probably got lonely or terribly hun- gry. I never did find out.

Anyway, the mere idea of a Big Sit seemed highly risible and mainly for weirdos.

In September, when Doug McRae suggests that he and I do a Big Sit at Presqu'ile Provincial Park, it seems eminently sensi- ble. Funny how things change. I am still stuck at 279 and a Big Sit will surely bring in a new species or two, especially with Doug's eyes. I will, of course, have to be very canny to make sure I don't make a fool of myself and have Doug find out just how deeply bogus I am. Let McRae call 'em, and keep the old gob shut. Don't be suckered into a quick misidentification of some easy bird.

"Only one thing, though," I say to Doug. "Is it okay to ask Margaret along? I think her nose might be out of joint if I don't at least ask her."

"Margaret? Of course! It would be great to have her along. What a blast that would be."

McRae is an enthusiast.

I call Margaret and give her the "I'm sure you won't be interested, but" line. She is interested. Big time. I don't know why I tease her.

The date is set for October 3.

I figure we will meet at the end of the campground and walk to Owen Point and select our viewing spot. Probably begin around 9:00 a.m., then see how we are doing in the afternoon before deciding how soon to knock it off. I call Doug to discuss details.

"Do you think if we meet in the park half an hour before sunrise it would be too late?" asks Doug. "Might get Great Horned or even Saw-whet before first light."

"You mean meet there around 5:00 or 5:30 a.m.?" I ask.

"Yeah, 'less of course you think that's a bit late," says Doug.

"Well," I say, "five-thirty's okay, but I wouldn't want to leave it any later."

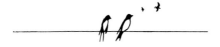

Five-thirty in the morning on October 3 finds Margaret and me in full rain gear staggering along the trail to Owen Point in the blackest darkness carrying chairs, scopes, and huge hampers of food. With Tymstra in mind I have gone heavy on the food, but I completely forgot a flashlight. Margaret and I stumble along in the dark, the halt leading the blind. My heart soars when I see a light out on Owen Point and it appears to be coming our way. No mugger in his right mind would be out at this ungodly hour. It's Doug, who has already gone out and got set up and is now coming back with a powerful flashlight to see if we need a hand — he quickly realizes his mistake.

We load McRae up and send him lurching ahead on the trail. I offer to carry his bins but pointedly do not insist that he call me "Boss Pope" henceforth.

Upon arrival, we decide on the best site, get ourselves organized and our chairs set up, and begin. Ta-dah: Ladies and Gentlemen — The Big Sit!

The owls betray us and even refuse to respond to Doug's shrieking Saw-whet tapes. Oh, well, as the Russians say, beginnings are a bad business. Things will look up.

They do, shortly after first light.

Doug espies a suspicious white form on the beach about thirty yards away and goes over to check it out. He is thrilled. It is a dead Sabine's Gull in almost perfect condition. I would have been slightly more thrilled with a live one, but this stiff is good enough for Doug. He talks a lot about putting it in his freezer, allegedly for Mark Peck, who collects avian corpses avidly. Doug looks forward to skinning it out tonight. I remember hearing somewhere that he eats the dead birds he finds, but this can scarcely be true, though his cousin, none other than

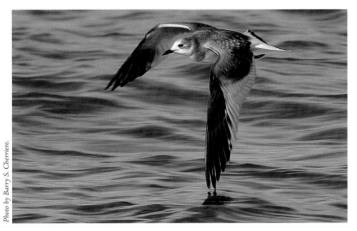

Sabine's Gull (juvenile). Fort Erie. Young birds like this are the ones we usually see in Southern Ontario in the autumn.

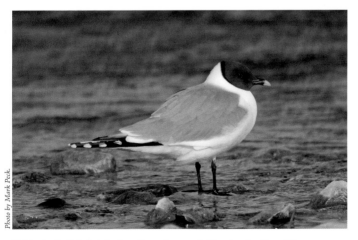

Sabine's Gull (adult in breeding plumage). Cambridge Bay, Nunavut. This is how they look on their breeding grounds.

John Carley, swears it is well-attested. Still, you have to wonder. He didn't bring a very big lunch. It's not every day you get to bird with the necrophagous. Bird carcasses remain a dominant leitmotif of Doug's conversation the rest of the day, arousing further suspicions.

As the morning warms up, I keep an eye on the Sabine's. It only has to twitch or move an eyelid and it is going on my list. I long for a cattle prod. But sadly the gull stays very dead. It is an ex-gull.

It is a slow day, but in the end we get fifty-five species, two of which are new for my year. I have somehow failed to see a **Peregrine Falcon** (280) all year, but here we have them buzzing around us all day; twelve sightings of at least five different birds.

In late morning, Doug spots the bird we have all being hoping we might see: a **jaeger — Parasitic** (281) as it turns out. I actually see the bird first but am damned if I am going to call a jaeger in front of Doug and Margaret and have it turn out to be a juvenile Herring Gull or something and then collapse in racking sobs on the sand as they spend the rest of the day saying it could have happened to anybody and how easy it is to confuse these two quite distinct birds. Another brush with fame missed. But we are all happy with a jaeger; especially Margaret and I, since we both *need* a jaeger. We knew they must go by Presqu'ile in October and are rewarded with two Parasitics by day's end.

The only mood-spoiler is watching birds die all around us of avian botulism at an alarming rate — well, alarming to the well-fed. A seemingly healthy Great Black-backed Gull flies in and lands well out in front of us. Four hours later its head is low to the water. Two more hours and its head and neck are on the water, and it is dead eight hours after it flew in. I restrain myself from saying to McRae, "Good eatin', I hear." I must not encourage morbid habits. A lone Greater Yellowlegs stands motionless all day and has not quite keeled over by the time we quit. I keep my eye on McRae. I am really partial to Greater Yellowlegs. Had it been a mere Lesser, I'd have said, "Bon appétit." Other ducks, gulls, and cormorants show varying degrees of distress as they slowly die. McRae feigns sorrow, obviously calculating how quickly he can get back after we leave. We can land on the moon, but seem unable to do much about this form of botulism.

Day's end is around dusk. I soon realize it would be pusillanimous in the extreme to suggest stopping after a mere twelve hours or so. Margaret and Doug are serious birders. You have to learn to suffer if you're going to play with the big leaguers. At least I'm not hungry, and carrying the coolers back to the car is a lot easier at the end of the day.

I am happy with two new species for a total of 281. Birds are coming with less frequency by early October. And the Big Sit is really fun. You certainly have lots of time to catch up on each other's news and the inside tales of the profession.

Try one; you might like it. Just be sure to sit well away from bushes and watch out for those guys with white coats and throw-nets that creep around all day trying to get close.

13

Closing the Gap

Ah, but a man's reach should exceed his grasp,
or what's a heaven for?

— ROBERT BROWNING, *ANDREA DEL SARTO*

GOTTA GO, GO, GO. THE day after The Big Sit, Hugh and I are
off in the early morning to Hamilton to try for Nelson's Sharp-
tailed Sparrow (now known as Nelson's Sparrow) at Cootes
Paradise. Margaret can't go and is very bitter. She knows Hugh
and I get the bird here every year and know just where to go.

We meet a birder on the way into the marsh who ecstati-
cally tells us that the Franklin's Gull has just flown the coop. I

do not say that I don't give a tinker's damn for the gull, but I want to. Badly.

Hugh and I go right to where we expect to find the sparrow and the bird is not there. Hughie becomes despondent. We proceed to the end of the trail, where the gull was, and where we have had Sharp-tailed before. We don't find either bird. The *Reisefuehrer's* mood darkens. We return to where we always get the sparrow for another try. A White Pelican flies right over us.

"Just our luck," says Hugh darkly. We saw hundreds of them in Rainy River. I ask him if he's having any fun at all, but he is not to be jollied out of his sombre mood.

We decide to try the chest-high grasses across the pond from our usual lucky spot and immediately have a **Nelson's Sharp-tailed** (282) pop up and sit for us for over a minute. The shadow of death lifts instantly. It is the best look Hugh has ever had of the sparrow, though he says this every year.

"That was a pretty neat pelican, wasn't it?" says Hugh on our way out.

I pay for this Sharp-tailed later. Margaret and I try for one repeatedly all around Cobourg. I really want to help her get one. She sends me through acres of beggar ticks and I ruin a number of pairs of socks before she finally gets the bird — in downtown Cobourg.

On October 9, Margaret and I rush off to Prince Edward Point. David Okines has reported a Myiarchus flycatcher that did not seem to be a Great Crested. Hugh is tied up with bridge but says darkly, "It's probably just an Ash-throated or a one-day wonder, but call me tonight if you find it and it's something

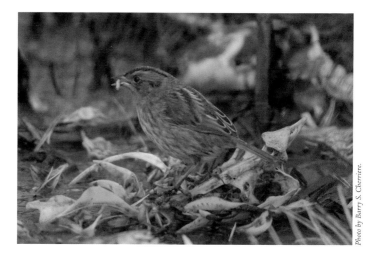

Photo by Barry S. Cherriere.

Nelson's Sharp-tailed Sparrow. Paradise Pond, Dundas Marsh. This bird came out of hiding in tall grass to eat grubs in the remains of a dead carp.

good." Ash-throated will be okay with me, I think to myself. But Margaret and I are to be thwarted. The bird is not there and oddly never shows up again. I say oddly, because usually such birds turn up again as soon as I leave the area. However, there are compensations. We get a Goshawk for Margaret and then we get a bird we both *need*: **Golden Eagle** (283). It is an immature bird and we are the first to get one this year. They don't start showing up regularly for another three weeks or so. This is but one of a number of birds that I find more attractive in juvenile plumage.

On October 10, Jim Fairchild phones to tell me he has just found a Hudsonian Godwit in Lynde Marsh. Margaret and I rush off the following day. The bird is not to be found from the viewing platform or the first trail into the marsh. We work our way south through impenetrable tangles, finding everything but Hudsonian. We do, however, spot the four Long-billed Dowitchers that Jim spoke of, and this spurs us on. We sink into black muck and I have to lift Margaret's right leg over the huge blown-down black willows, but she soldiers on, fearful lest I get the bird up ahead without her. It is a long walk back for Margaret. My walk seems short because Margaret points out a Cackling Goose flying right over us with a bunch of Canadas. I *need* **Cackling Goose** (284), even if she does not. It is another bird I did not bother to go see when it was available (in the Cobourg Harbour in January) because I was so sure I'd see tons later.

October 12 finds the intrepid team of Dave Beadle, Currie, and Pope heading west to the OFO Convention at Point Pelee. I have high hopes for this weekend, especially since we have Beadle with us. If something peeps, Beadle will be all over it.

We stop at Hillman's Marsh on the way into town. A woman in the parking lot has just seen several hundred Soras or some such thing, and my hopes fly high. I still *need* Sora and Orange-crowned Warbler. We set up for rails and something tiny flits away out of a shrub and instantly disappears. Beadle asks, "You still need Orange-crowned?"

"Big time," I say.

"Well, that was an Orange-crowned just now," says Dave. I am about to say, "yeah, sure," but remembering it's Beadle I'm with, I race off after the bird. Guess what? **Orange-crowned Warbler** (285) — an auspicious beginning, even if there wasn't a Sora within miles.

October 13 and still no bloody Sora, though I hang around marshes all day. Spikey Pike tells us they are still around out in the pond where he has been in his canoe. There is hope. No new bird today. Hope fades.

On October 14 my only request is to start out the day early at the Marsh Boardwalk. To humour me, the others agree. We walk out seventy metres and I find a **Sora** (286) warming up in the first morning sun and get it in my new Zeiss scope at fifty power. Nicest Sora *I* ever saw. Even Dave is impressed.

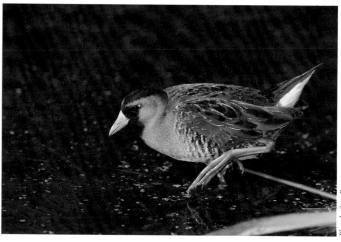

Sora. Red Bay, north of Wiarton. These feet were made for skittering around on lily pads.

Closing the Gap

To quell the *Reisefuehrer*'s whining about geese, Dave and I agree to a quick side trip out to Jack Miner's where Hugh hopes for Snow Goose, Ross's, and Greater White-fronted. He spurns my road map and navigates by memory. We see a lot of countryside. The *Reisefuehrer* sinks rapidly into the Slough of Despond. Finally, after humiliating himself by asking directions, we arrive at the Sanctuary, which is closed. Beadle generously points out nine Canada Geese grazing in the field across from the gate. Hugh does not respond. I remind him of Beadle's First Law: One tends to see a good bird after some major cock-up. He is not cheered. Only some big rarity is going to pull him out of this. I ask Dave what he wants to do. He says he would like to see something really good. Who wouldn't? Hugh and I still *need* Western Sandpiper, so we decide to go to Blenheim Sewage lagoons on the way home. You never know.

It turns out not to be an error.

When we hit the Blenheim lagoons, Dave and Hugh head in immediately. By the grace of God I am detained for a minute at the car, and just before I head off to catch up with them, I see a vehicle screech to a stop and Ron Tozer jumps out and starts telling people something. I think I hear a bird mentioned, but know it can't be what I think, so I wait till Ron walks up and says, "Jim [James T.] Burk has found a Wheatear at Shrewsbury."

Beadle and Currie are stopped dead in their tracks by my yell. By my gesticulations they know something is up and come back with due celerity. Seconds later we are fishtailing down the road, heading for Shrewsbury with the *Reisefuehrer* calling out short-cut directions. Even Dave is excited. It will be a first for him in Ontario as it will for me. We have got to get this bird.

As we scream up, there are some twenty people milling about. What the hell is the matter with them? No one is looking.

"Is the Wheatear gone?" I ask, heart sinking into my boots.

"It's just down over the bank for a moment," says the closest birder. Suddenly, up it pops, hawking for a huge cicada-like insect. It then lands nine metres away and spends the next ten minutes trying to dispatch and consume said insect. I get the **Northern Wheatear** (287) in my scope at high power and it is, as they now say, awesome.

John Carley arrives and sees the bird, and I find I am genuinely glad for him. I am going soft. I am worried about Margaret, though, who left for home before we did. I borrow a phone to call her, but the guy beside me tells me Margaret was here half an hour ago and saw this bird. Great, I won't have to play it down for her and tell her it was just another bird and not to worry about missing this one just like the one she looked so hard for but failed to find on Wolfe Island last week. Hughie is ecstatic and all thoughts of the Jack Miner debacle are banished from his mind. Dave and I are equally ecstatic getting a new Ontario bird. The trip home is quite jolly. I am at 287 and possibly on a roll.

After nearly killing ourselves at Lynde Creek and elsewhere, Margaret and I, albeit on different days, finally get **Hudsonian Godwit** (288) on October 14–15 at Coot's Pond, Darlington. Margaret and everyone else find it easily at the west end of the pond, right where it's supposed to be. The morning I go, the thing decides to hide for a while in deep reeds. I rush down to the east end in desperation. I look everywhere. Obviously I am to be the first to miss this bird. As I walk back dejectedly, I notice a Hudsonian Godwit casually feeding at the west end, right out in the open about eight metres from me. The bird winks and appears to perform a slight salaam — Gotcha! — though the uninitiated might think it is just scratching its head. Birds do have a sense of humour, you know, and anyone who has birded extensively knows they can be perverse. This bird gave me a bit of a scare before relenting.

14

Floating Jaegers

Confusion now hath made his masterpiece.

— SHAKESPEARE, *MACBETH*, ACT II

I KNOW FOR CERTAIN THAT to get to three hundred, one has to get things like all three jaegers and spend some time at Van Wagner's Beach. That is practically axiomatic. I also know that the best time for Long-tailed Jaeger is late August/ early September.

Somehow it is more than halfway through October and I have only been over at Van Wagner's once. How can this be? I go more than once even when I am not doing a Big Year. Am

I not serious about hitting three hundred? I've already missed the Long-tailed; do I want to miss Parasitic and Pomarines, as well?

I phone Margaret and we begin our vigil on the meretricious weather websites, waiting for strong east winds. We both *need* Pomarine Jaeger and she *needs* Sabine's Gull in addition. October 16 is to be the day. Early in the morning we are on our way. The last thing I want is to get there at noon and hear from all the Hamilton gang that while jaeger activity has been ferocious all morning, matched only by rare gulls and shearwaters, it seems to have dropped off utterly during the last half hour and is doubtless over for the day.

Margaret and I arrive early. There are only two or three diehards there, Norm Murr and Dave Don among them. We set up. I begin to stare hard, prepared to continue for at least twelve hours unless I get jaegered out earlier. A few other birders straggle in, among them Barry Cherriere and Cheryl Edgecombe. For a long time I see nothing. But neither does Cherriere, so there's nothing out there.

Suddenly, I see it. A big dark-morph Pomarine Jaeger. Funny no one else has seen it yet. I call it. "Big dark Pommie, coming in from the north, quite far out." I keep up the directions, as is expected. "Floating in about ten o'clock, up fairly high, a scope frame above the horizon, peeling off, starting to dive down toward the water in a slow floating arc, quite low now."

It seems odd that no one else has seen it yet. It's a dandy, dark adult. I keep up the patter. "Right down on the water now, hovering, starting to go back up just the way it came, higher

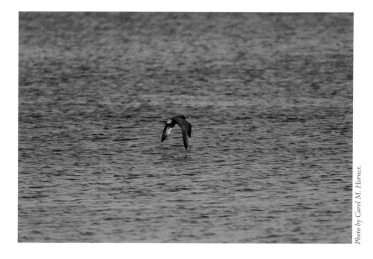

Pomarine Jaeger (juvenile). Lake Simcoe. After entanglement with fish hooks and line, this bird eventually died.

and higher, peeling left." It is at this moment I have a disheartening revelation. This is no jaeger. It's a bloody floater! For the younger set (the under-eighties), floaters are those things that lazily drift across your eyes in larger sizes and ever increasing numbers as you age. There is even such a thing as a floater shower — of great interest only to ophthalmologists. Can you imagine thirty to forty jaegers whipping around in your scope? Bruce Falls says it happens all the time.

Anyway, what do I do now? Make a clean breast of it, or say I've suddenly lost it on the horizon in the chop and heat shimmer? Could I stand having Barry and Cheryl think I am any more bogus than I actually am? And what if Cherriere says,

"I'm outta here if this guy is going to stay." Though a scrupulously honest person, I am unable to emulate George Washington. They know I am lying but are very good about it and let on that it was their fault they couldn't get on to the bird. Margaret, on the other hand, who would have seen a House Fly at two kilometres, gives me a very odd look. She is a doctor.

Half an hour later, I see another jaeger, very high and very far off, kind of hovering and fighting the wind. I watch the bastard to make sure it isn't another treacherous floater trying to make a fool out of me. This one is definitely a bird. Finally, I mention it. Barry casually says, "It's a Short-eared Owl; been there all morning."

That's it. I'm never calling another bird. I am devastated, my non-existent reputation in shambles. What's a frigging owl doing hovering high over Lake Ontario in thirty-kilometre winds? No one knows, but he remains there all day. I take a strong disliking to marine owls.

I vow to keep my gob firmly shut for the rest of the day. I don't care if an albatross appears; I'm not saying anything. Half an hour later a big dark lumbering jaeger chases a smaller, more agile Parasitic Jaeger across the bay right out in front of us. "**Pomarine Jaeger!**" (289) Margaret and I both yell. I have learned nothing, but at least it *is* a Pomarine Jaeger. We see several more during the day and a few more Parasitics, and at one point a Black-legged Kittiwake flies up and lands right in front of us on the beach.

Then things quiet down, though floater action is terrific. Cherriere stares silently through his scope without surcease.

Though I have terrible eye fatigue, I don't want to appear frivolous in front of Barry and Cheryl. I stare on in a trance. Suddenly, Barry yells "Sabine's Gull." I force myself to look, even though I don't really *need* it. I immediately see it. Margaret, who *needs* it, does not. This worries me. I have to drive home with her and I hate to see adults cry. Barry continues the patter and, thank God, Margaret sees the bird. I am happy for her. No, really. When this altruism kicked in, I don't know. I may be ill. But we are now in this together and I really want her to make three hundred, too. Besides, it is only fair; it was Barry who found me my Sabine's Gull way back on September 8.

It was a good day, almost a perfect day, if only it hadn't been for the damn floaters.

15

No Peace for the Wicked

I can't horse around here all day.

— IMPATIENT TWITCHER IN TEXAS

A POSSIBLE WHITE-FACED IBIS turns up in Hamilton. Margaret and I wait for a picture that shows its red eye and then, on October 20, we race off to Dundas Marsh. As we burst forth from the five-metre-high phragmites, I see Roy Smith and Winnie Poon in a group of people. Are they looking dejected or triumphant? If the bird is there, why isn't Winnie photographing it? Several people are talking about a nearby Cackling Goose. Cackling shmackling. "Where's the bloody ibis?" I am about to ask in a most forceful manner, when I notice it placidly feeding nearby. It is indeed a **White-faced Ibis** (290), and we get long, delicious looks at it. Eventually I even condescend to glance at the Cackling Goose; a nice little bird, but it doesn't even have red eyes.

Some might consider my impatience ungentlemanly and bordering on the churlish. I myself have always mocked birders who suddenly arrive and demand to be told immediately exactly where some bird is. An old birding friend from Pelee I haven't seen in years, Al Patterson, used to tell a wonderful story. He was birding somewhere in Texas by himself, not far from a road. A guy in a huge Cadillac convertible screams up, stops, and yells to Al, "Have ya got the bird?"

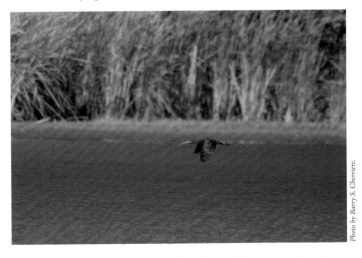

Photo by Barry S. Cherriere.

White-faced Ibis. Hydro Pond, Dundas Marsh. Having missed the few preceding records, this bird was a first for me in Ontario.

Al naively asks, "Which bird?"

"The Beardless Tyrannulet," the guy yells.

"Well," says Al, "I think I saw—"

"Look," says the guy, "you either seen the bird or you ain't. I can't horse around all day."

After seeing the ibis, for the first time I have an understanding of this story that entails less scorn and mockery. I think of the time I was looking for the Razorbill in late 2006 at Niagara-on-the-Lake. Nobody had seen it in the waves for several hours and finally a lady spotted it.

"Where? Where?" everybody starts yelling.

"Well, there's a boat in the background," she says, still looking through her scope.

There are scores of boats fishing for salmon all around the area.

"Which boat?" we all cry.

"Well, it's blue," says the lady.

There are four or five blue boats.

"Which blue boat?" we cry.

"Well, there are two guys in it …"

"Look," says my neighbour, a chap from London whose name, let us say, escapes me at the moment, "just tell us where the f*****g bird is? Is that too much to ask?"

He said exactly what I was thinking. I understood it deeply. Fortunately, we all quickly got onto the bird before more urgent questions were asked. Birding can be bad for the blood pressure, you know. I won't even mention the tense hours spent trying to coax the thing across the centre of the river so we could count it as an Ontario bird. ("Here, Razorbill. Here, Razorbill. Good bird. No, you idiot, this way!") Rarities love to hug the New York side of the river.

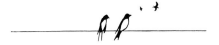

I have already mentioned my intense *schadenfreude* when Margaret missed the Ross's Goose on October 22. My joy at her seeing the ibis with me does not yet extend to having her knock off good birds without me. On October 23, the two of us head for Reesor Pond, determined to find the Ross's if we have to wait all day. It is teeming rain and no white geese are on the pond. Off to the north we see geese flying, and it looks like there are a few Snows among them. We see where they seem to land and set off to check them out. After a literal wild goose chase — the term has far more meaning for me now — we try one last road and see a mixed flock of Canadas and some Snows feeding in corn stubble right near the road. We stop and, without even getting out of the car, see a little **Ross's Goose** (291) looking at us shyly with its innocent and fetching eyes; a lovely little bird. Nothing mean about it like with some Canadas. It is oblivious to the driving rain and we study it as we eat a leisurely lunch. We are partial to Ross's Geese.

October 28 is a red-letter day for me. I get a freebie without even moving from my house. Without even looking out the window. No, a rarity does not come down the chimney. The phone rings. It's Margaret. She tells me that the OBRC has finally decided to put **Trumpeter Swan** (292) on the list of allowable Ontario birds, given that there is a large well-established breeding colony around the lower Great Lakes and has been for some time. Neither of us has to rush out and try to see one; we saw them repeatedly in Cobourg Harbour in the winter. This is my easiest bird all year with the possible exception of House Sparrow in our back hall. I see nothing strange about the fact that Margaret heads the OBRC and chooses this moment to heatedly press Trumpeter Swan's case. Science is science and truth will out. She couldn't help it. The timing just happened to work in our favour. And contrary to sly innuendoes and mean-spirited murmurings, no money changed hands, though I was more than willing to help out on this front. Not a glorious way to get a bird, but as Hughie says, hey, it's a tick. True, John Carley kicked up a terrible fuss and hinted that inclusion of Trumpeter Swan would compromise my whole endeavour, but his views changed magically when he realized that he, too, could now include it on his all-time Ontario list, and I heard no more grumblings. I view it as the OBRC payback for not letting me use Northern Bobwhite.

The phantom Eurasian Wigeon starts showing up again at the Dupont pond in Kingston. It wants to sucker me down yet again and have a good giggle. Well, it's not getting this boy again. Who cares if Bruce Di Labio has seen it eighty-six times and considers it the most reliable bird in Ontario. I have chased this Kingston bird seven times and missed others all over the province, as well. I read classical literature and I recognize nemesis when I see it. This is my nemesis bird for 2007. Last year it was a garbage bird for me. Had to flee them at Lee Brown's Pond; it was Alfred Hitchcock all over again. Never went to Hillman's Marsh or Cranberry Marsh in '06 without seeing one tooling around on the far shore. But this year? Forget it.

The first time Hugh and I went after the Kingston bird was in early January. It had been seen reliably in the Dupont pond, so we went for it. We arrived early. It was minus thirty degrees Celsius, but only if you completely discounted the raging wind. And it had snowed hard in the night. There were several thousand ducks on the pond, all with their heads buried deeply under their wings and with ten-centimetre triangles of snow rising neatly on their bodies. We peered for half an hour into the swirling mists above this heated pond but during this time not one duck even partially eased his head out for a look, even though the *Reisefuehrer* used every trick in his book, including the famous flapping flight simulation that works wonders with gulls and astounds passing psychiatrists. He began to mutter darkly about it being so cold that all the stones are frozen to the ground. I knew it was time to get him back into the car. We don't even know if they were Mallards or wigeon, or Purple Gallinules for that matter.

I went back several times alone during the next few days. One day I looked at over five hundred American Wigeon in the surrounding area and conceived a powerful dislike for wigeons in general. I'd rather look at bastard Mallards racing for the bread loaf in Cobourg Harbour any day. Even Long Point failed me with both Hugh and Margaret on separate trips.

No Peace for the Wicked

So when Margaret calls on October 29 and says we have to go to Kingston and get the now reappearing Eurasian, I am less than enthusiastic. But I can't say no because Margaret doesn't even *need* the bird and she is determined to help me. Of course, when we arrive the bird is not in the pond. Surprise. While Margaret is scouring the water for other ducks, for something to do I begin scoping a large flock of ducks beyond the pond in the bay. I suddenly see a Eurasian Wigeon and shout with unrestrained joy and glee. I show it to Margaret who is uncharacteristically unenthusiastic and mumbles something about hybrids under her breath. I look again and, sure enough, something is not right. It is a bloody hybrid Eurasian/American — and uncountable. Margaret tries to rally me by talking about how interesting it is to see this bird, but I am neither interested nor consoled. It's not a tick. I stifle my racking sobs — the ABA considers it unmanly to cry in the field and most crack birders wait until they are safely at home in their bedrooms — and carry on bitterly scoping American Wigeon in the large flock. But there is a bird god — not often benevolent, I admit — and I find the real **Eurasian Wigeon** (293) almost immediately. The decision was made that I had suffered enough and paid the going price and the bird was delivered unto me.

The beat goes on. A Pacific Loon is reported on Ontbirds off Oshawa Second Marsh, and Margaret and I are up with the hens to see it next morning, November 3. The good news is that the lake is calm. The bad news is that there are hundreds of Common and Red-throated Loons out there and we are alone. We hit several suspicious birds but nothing we can honestly make into a Pacific, until we finally settle on one bird and really give it a going over. Though distant, it eventually — no doubt grudgingly — yields up all its field signs. It is a **Pacific Loon** (294). Seeing our body language, Jim Fairchild, who has been taking his time coming toward us up the beach, breaks into a run.

"Have you got the Pacific?"

"It's in my scope, Jim."

Jim has a good look and we all congratulate ourselves and leave. Later, no one re-finds this bird. They don't show themselves to just anybody.

Keeping the roll going is important. Bohemian Waxwings are showing up all over and Margaret and I *need* one. The latest

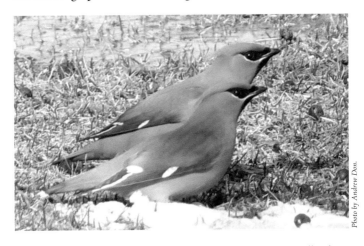

Photo by Andrew Don.

Bohemian Waxwings. Simcoe. These restless travellers love small red crab apples.

report has them way up at Willow Beach on Lake Simcoe. We decide to go for it on November 4, assuming we will almost certainly get Bohemian on the way and probably Pine Grosbeak to boot. We don't. We drive all over the proverbial hell's half acre en route and nary a waxwing. It is on this trip that my strong dislike of Fall Webworm really crystallizes into intense hatred. Who would invent an insect that makes nests that look just like birds after the leaves are down? They can weave waxwings (both Cedar and Bohemian) and kingbirds, and they do a mean Pine Grosbeak. Fortunately, few are good enough to do raptors and I have only seen one creditable screech-owl. They have run amok in Ontario this fall. It's perverse. By the time we hit Willow Beach we have more or less thrown in the towel. We drive down the side streets in despair and see a tree full of birds that are not starlings. They appear to be waxwings. We open the window and hear quiet trilling. **Bohemian Waxwings** (295)! — thirty-five to be exact. We are happy to get these marauders and vagrants because one can so easily miss them. Pine Grosbeaks are a much easier bird to find, especially if you are not cursed.

16

So Close, and Yet So Far

Rag of a man that I am, is this the end of me?
— Odysseus in Homer's *The Odyssey*

On November 4, when I got Bohemian Waxwing as bird 295, I figured three hundred was a cakewalk. How could I miss? I even started telling people that I thought I was going to make it — just a matter of time. The gods, of course, were setting me up for the fall. Had I not heard of hubris? Humpty Dumpty syndrome? I should have known better. I've been a loser all my life. Why should I start to come through now? Had I done anything other than offer constant, often copious, libations each evening to gain favour with the bird god? I should have seen it coming.

I spend hours in the field day after day, but no new birds. It is a bleak and desperate November. Even the Internet is reporting few novelties and the ones it does post manage to avoid me no matter how soon I chase off after them. My sole comfort is that Margaret and Hugh are not racing ahead scoring right and left and leaving me struggling in their wake. This is another doldrums period. The whole province is quiet.

And I still can't find Pine Grosbeak. I've been missing them everywhere, while everyone else has been having really good luck with them. I get sick of crabapples and buckthorn; I check every one within miles of Cobourg. It is embarrassing. People

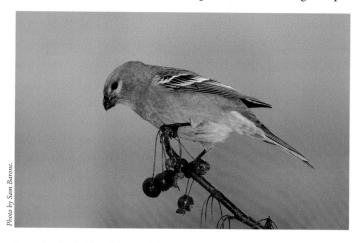

Photo by Sam Barone.

Pine Grosbeak (female). Guelph. Less gaudy than the male, to be sure, but this female looked awfully good to me.

are discussing and comparing all the Pines they are seeing; others are bored with Pines — too numerous.

Eventually, I am the only person in the province who has failed to see one of these ubiquitous invaders, which as Ron Pittaway predicted, would be all over the place in goodly numbers. I'd all but counted the bird as a given. Imagine my horror when I understand it is going to be the Eurasian Wigeon all over again, but this time with a less felicitous outcome. The gods have lost patience with the Rewards for Hard Work Program and have reverted to their old ways. Screw Pope wherever possible without hurting other birders unduly. There is one other birder, a rookie junior field naturalist in Punkeydoodles Corners who has also failed to see Pine Grosbeak, but he has been ill. It is understandable. People are cutting him some slack.

Then, on November 20, Don Shanahan calls to say there is a flock of Pine Grosbeaks outside the Brighton Beer Store. I do not stop to ponder how Don might have come to find them. These things happen. Margaret (who has already seen one yesterday and knows from experience that loser Pope will never find one without her) and I are off in a flash. As we arrive, I see a flock of birds explode out of a nearby tree, gain height, and fly as if possessed for the horizon. I know they are Pine Grosbeaks, but I do not get my diagnostic look. A lesser man and one not so used to defeat and abject disappointment might have wept. I begin to stare above my head into dark, forbidding spruce trees. As I stand in the sad bleak silence thinking of Cato the Younger in the crepuscular gloom, Margaret says, "Oh, what was that?"

"What was what?" I ask, as I so often do around Margaret. She has heard some little cheep or tweet or something, maybe a distant Brown Creeper clearing its throat.

"There, that call," says Margaret. "Isn't that Pine Grosbeak?"

"Right on," I say, hearing nothing except the now-alluring creak of the Beer Store door. Then the fates play another trick on me. I think I hear a Greater Yellowlegs. It seems unlikely that this species hides in fir trees in the winter, but I know enough to start screening those fir trees madly. Right above us, hidden deep in the branches of a big spruce, we see the saffron rump and then the whole body of a beautiful female **Pine Grosbeak** (296), the most beautiful one of these unprepossessing birds I have ever seen.

Ticky, ticky.

17

299 and 300 — Sort Of

I am an ass.

— Dogberry, in Shakespeare's
Much Ado about Nothing, Act IV

Somehow, during the desperate days between November 4 and November 20, when I was stuck at 295, I had somehow begun to factor in my heard-only birds and to start thinking I had 297. This would give me a much better chance of hitting three hundred. I mean, by ABA rules this was really my true number and this could save me from embarrassing failure. Though I would always know I was a true loser, other people would think I had made it. So, with Pine Grosbeak I was at 298; not a hopeless position like 296. Two more birds and I'm a winner ABA style and that will at least be something. Stop people from saying, "Yeah, poor bugger, he tried so hard. Raced all over the province and still couldn't do it. A loser, eh?"

On the evening of November 20, I note on Ontbirds that someone has found a Yellow-breasted Chat in the park at Ashbridge's Bay. Imagine! I long since gave up all hope for a chat after missing it for the first time in years at both Point Pelee and Pelee Island.

Nonetheless, plucky little devil, on the morning of November 21, in driving freezing rain, I head for Toronto alone to try for the chat in fullest comprehension of the certainty of defeat. The quicker after a posting, the better, regardless of the weather.

It was found in the extreme southwest part of the park. I repeat this to myself as a kind of mantra all the way to Ashbridge's Bay, get out of the car, don warm clothes and raingear, and set off almost at a run directly to the extreme southeast corner of the park, where I search for a full hour. Lots of good habitat — I even find the mentioned euonymus bush with red berries, though it is not exactly where the posting suggested — but no chat. But I am damned if I am going to give up. I stop to regroup and clarify my thoughts.

"What do I know?" I ask myself.

A voice says, "The bird is in the extreme southwest corner of the park."

"Exactly," I say.

"Then why are you in the extreme southeast corner, you fool," the voice continues.

Hmm. An excellent question. It *is* mystifying and would break a lesser man. I rush over to the southwest corner, and find the red euonymus berries right where they should be, and search diligently for thirty minutes. Of course, in the freezing rain no one else appears to help. Just before giving up, I decide to give pishing a whirl and immediately hear a responsive chip right beside me, then another. I look madly about. It has to be the chat. What else in its right mind would be out here? Suddenly, perhaps divinely inspired, I glance up, and there, six metres over my head, feeding placidly in a Russian Olive, is Mr. Chat. The bird is in gorgeous plumage, just like at Pelee, and seemingly unaware of the freezing rain. **Yellow-breasted Chat** (297/299) is another sweet bird, a favourite at any time, but particularly so now — under the circumstances, absolutely thrilling.

Soaked to the hide and numb with cold, I stagger back to the car and head home. I stop only to phone Felicity to say I have found the chat, but will be very late for lunch. Almost before I speak, she says breathlessly, "Margaret has just phoned to say the Northern Gannet is back in Cobourg Harbour."

Say no more. I have already missed this elusive bird several times. I run back to the car, floor it, and head for Cobourg, insouciantly passing the signs promising thousands of dollars of fines and jail time for all heavy speeders. I drive like the people who usually make me so mad, but this is, of course, completely different. I have just cause. I think about how easy it was for Felicity several days ago when Joan and Barbara came

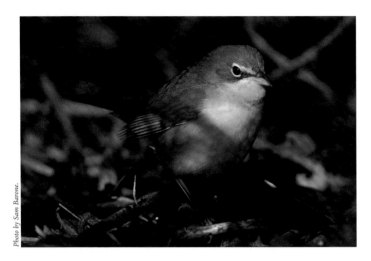

Photo by Sam Barone.

Yellow-breasted Chat. Ashbridge's Bay, Toronto. On this sleety late November day this bird does not look as cold as I was.

for lunch in my absence and they all went down to the harbour and watched a gannet swoop and dive and play silly buggers just off the pier. It was a challenge to seem pleased about that, I can tell you.

On the way to the harbour, racing along Albert Street, I see Margaret's car in her driveway. I stop in.

"Have you seen it?" asks Margaret. "I waited an hour keeping track of it but got too cold and I had to come home."

She carefully describes where she last saw it — flying out into the lake, away from the feeding frenzy of mergs, loons, and gulls — and with no hope at all, I race to the harbour, run out on the headland, and get the scope going.

Loons, hundreds of bastardly loons, swarms of big dark first-winter Herring Gulls, and two thousand Red-breasted Mergs. How could one find the gannet in this mob? Then I remember it flew out from the frenzy into the lake. I make a sweep at low power and there it is, all by its lonesome, seemingly in lordly disdain of the feeding flock. I watch it for half an hour, fingers and eye freezing to my scope, before it flies right in before me and begins to dive and feed actively. **Northern Gannet** (298/300). A worthy fowl! Not like my hundredth bird my first time at Churchill which was a rare (in Churchill) House Sparrow.

By everyone else's rules this is my number three hundred. It *feels* like three hundred. Margaret and Felicity and I go out for dinner this night and a bottle or two dies. According to Felicity, Margaret and I talk almost the whole time about birds, though I personally doubt it.

Now I have to get number three hundred for Margaret. I feel bad being there first. I had somehow thought we would both get number three hundred simultaneously. And she helped so much near the end. And besides, I *really* need two more birds to accomplish what I set out to do according to my rules. I am still not where I want to be.

It will be! It will be!

18

299 and 300 — In Sooth

"O frabjous day! Callooh! Callay!" He chortled in his joy.

— LEWIS CARROLL, *JABBERWOCKY*

NEAR THE END OF NOVEMBER, Margaret and I decide to make abortive trip number three thousand to Presqu'ile for Purple Sandpipers. The Cobourg waterfront is failing to produce even though they are being seen elsewhere in the province. She is stuck at 299 and is quite desperate.

When I arrive at her house, there is a flock of redpolls at her famous feeders, and she says to come and have a look. One of them is rather whitish and pale by comparison to the others.

We have a pretty good look and see a whitish rump, little or no streaking under the tail, minimal streaking on the sides, and an overall paleness compared to the other birds. The whole flock whisks away before we are completely finished with bill and cap, et cetera. We both feel quite sure it was a Hoary, but decide it would be somehow unsatisfactory to count it as Margaret's number three hundred. We agree to count it if we don't get a different three hundredth bird, and if we do get another, we will consider Hoary Redpoll her 301st. Even when, shortly after, we see the photos of the two first-year female Hoaries banded on Leslie Street Spit and realize our bird was one of the same, we stick by our decision. Like me, Margaret does not want any soft birds on her list.

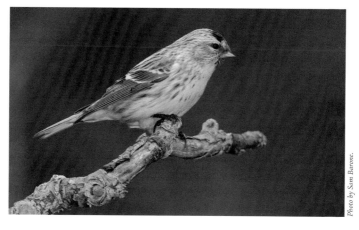

Photo by Sam Barone.

"Southern" Hoary Redpoll (exilipes). Mississauga. A relatively pale, rather faintly streaked bird with heavy feathering at the base of the small, stubby bill.

Presqu'ile betrays us yet again. And it is so windy I practically have to load Margaret down with stones. When crossing the tombolo, I am glad she does not have an umbrella: Shades of Mary Poppins. Eventually I leave her in the duck blind at the beginning of Gull Island and fight my way around the whole island to make sure there are no Purple Sands rejoicing in some particularly devious hidey hole. Fortunately, I don't find any, because I don't know how I would get her out to see them, though we would definitely try. What with the metre-high waves, Margaret does not make me go out to Sebastopol Island as usual. Thank God for small mercies. We come home with our tails between our legs.

Over the next week we do everything possible to get her number three hundred. We even stay overnight in Niagara-on-the-Lake so we can have multiple tries at King Eider in Burlington, Hawk Owl at Port Weller, Purple Sandpiper at Niagara, and Black-headed Gull at Fort Erie. Swells nearly one metre high make it impossible to find the eider; the Hawk Owl flies the coop even though we are there fifteen hours after it was seen by Hugh; the Black-headed Gull is not seen by anybody; and they even go so far as to raise the water a foot at Niagara and flood the rocks and islands to deny us Purple Sandpiper. I'd like to get my hands on the person who tipped them off about our arrival. The dreadful ice-storm and weather warning is only an additional background irritant for us — one more minor cross to bear.

All our hopes are now on a planned Big Day with Doug McRae on December 4. As usual, Doug wants to start at least an hour before dawn to try for owls. Somehow we talk him into starting from his house only half an hour before dawn. After a short period of abortive owling, we decide to work Presqu'ile and the lakeshore before heading inland. Doug is well aware of Margaret's desperate *need* for Purple Sandpiper.

After a few good birds — the best of which is Fred Helleiner's personal Carolina Wren, which actually sings for us at minus ten degrees Celsius — we decide to go directly for Purple Sandpiper, not the least reason being the fact that Margaret has talked about nothing else all morning. She has them on the brain. They have been visiting her a lot of late in her dreams. Doug found four on Gull Island two days before, so we have a decent chance. The problem is logistical; everything is coated with ice after the storm — skating rinks are like sand

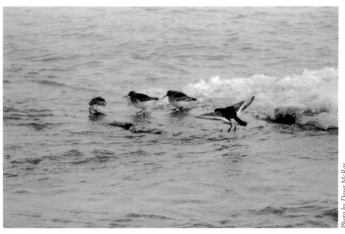

Purple Sandpipers (juveniles). Presqu'ile Provincial Park. We nearly got killed approaching these birds over the rugged, glassy December ice.

by comparison — and the wind is absolutely raging at Owen Point. Margaret frequently goes up on her heels in preparation for takeoff on the way to the point, so we decide to leave her there on the point at a duck blind with the 60-power scope while Doug and I stagger out to the island over the tombolo.

It is slow-going and treacherous, but we both know there is no turning back. Who wants to spend the good part of a day with someone slashed by the sharp knives of failure and despair? Even without scopes it is tough-going. At one point I fear McRae is losing more than his footing when he inexplicably breaks out into a Celtic dancing routine in his hip waders. First time I've seen the sword dance in ages. I know he has a Scottish surname, but I had no idea he was so deeply into Scottish nationalism and culture. Dostoevsky wrote that "another's soul is a darkness," meaning that you never know what lies beneath the surface in another person. Am I having a Dostoevskian moment? No, McRae is out of control and trying to stay upright. This is neither ebullience nor a display of nationalism.

When we finally get to the island, we realize the birds are either going to have to be at the first point, or we are going to have to leave them be like the Ruddy Turnstone reputed to be out on Sebastopol. Walking the whole of Gull Island is out of the question. Greater love hath no man than to lay down his life for a bird and all that, but there are limits.

Rounding the point is treacherous and, as we gradually see farther and farther around it, we both figure we're out of luck. But lo and behold, magically, on the edge of a limestone rock formation, are four fat Purple Sandpipers feeding merrily and utterly unconcerned by our arrival.

I turn and signal to Margaret, hoping she is watching and can see me, and begin pointing down in front of me. No reaction, though she appears glued to the scope. Then we move forward and the birds make a little two-metre flight up from the water's edge and land on top of the flat rock. I look back, frantically pointing, and see a diminutive figure in the distance glued to a scope, right hand raised triumphantly in a closed-fisted victory salute. I tell Doug, "I think she's seen them."

At this point Doug slips and slides his way to the water and gets around behind the birds in his waders to take some smashing photos of the birds (one of which is later presented to Margaret), after which we leave them to feed undisturbed.

Purple Sandpiper is Margaret's bird number three hundred and Hoary Redpoll becomes 301. As for me, I count **Hoary Redpoll** as my number 299 seen and **Purple Sandpiper** as my number three hundred seen, sealed, and delivered. I love these portly birds — a wonderful choice for my true three-hundredth. Watching them feed and swim about like phalaropes in icy seas is an incredible sight. I take my hat off to them.

The rest of our Big Day seems joyous and unstrained. Even the owls treat us better and we have an Eastern Screech-Owl flying all around our heads at dusk just before calling it a day. Sadly, Hugh is not there when we find Bohemian Waxwings in the very tree we took him and Bruce Falls to several days before.

Oddly, getting my three-hundredth seen bird was not as thrilling for me as getting number three hundred ABA style, and I understood why Margaret was so ecstatic about her three-hundredth bird.

The pressure, entirely self-imposed to be sure, but nonetheless real, was suddenly off. Birding could be sheer pleasure again. New species would be the gravy now.

Oh, joy!

19

Gravy Birds

Onwards, ever onwards!

— Fast Eddy Phibbs

THE INNOCENT JOY OF SEEING three hundred birds does not last as long as I expected.

"Sure hope they don't lump Thayer's Gull with Iceland," says Carley darkly after I mention getting my three hundredth.

I suddenly realize that just as easily as the powers that be had given me a bird — Trumpeter Swan — they could take one or two away. I had remembered splitting, but forgotten lumping. In police and underworld jargon, lumping and splitting, I'm led to believe, is used when a criminal whacks someone over the head and then flees the scene of the crime. Lumping, though perhaps not splitting, I would submit, is a crime in the birding world. I'd like to get my hands on the guy who is going around claiming all white-headed gulls are really the same species. We could all lose a pile there. These damn bird committees have too much power. I lost Cassin's Vireo on my Ontario life list two years ago because of a committee — in this case the OBRC — not that I am bitter or anything. It becomes clear to me that I need a cushion of at least one and perhaps two birds to make sure my three hundred will stand. Oh, dear. And here for five whole days I had been trying to have a life again. Now it's back into the breach, dear friends.

Hugh still *needs* some birds to make three hundred. He is substantially behind because of his four weeks in Peru. We decide to head to Niagara on December 10 with five target birds in mind: Hawk Owl, King Eider, Black-headed Gull, Purple Sandpiper, and Little Gull. He does not *need* Hawk Owl, but I do, having missed the Port Weller bird. I don't *need* Purple Sandpiper, but Hugh does. Things start brilliantly, at least from my point of view. We get the **Northern Hawk Owl** (301) easily at Stoney Creek, right on the telephone wires beside the road. Even at this early stage, the bird is already being harassed by idiots who have not yet discovered digiscoping. Ironically, it later turns out that this is the very bird Margaret and I missed at Port Weller, which has moved on to better voling country.

We should have gone straight home after this little victory.

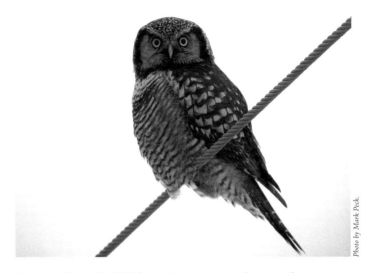

Photo by Mark Peck.

Northern Hawk Owl. Welcome. In my opinion this is our fiercest-looking owl.

We hit the Burlington lakefront, but spot no King Eider, male or female. "Batting fifty-fifty," says Hugh. "That's not too bad. Let's head straight to Fort Erie and knock off the Black-headed Gull. Then we can pick up Purple Sand at the Falls and probably Little Gull, as well, though if we miss it there we can always get it at Adam Beck or Queenston. Could get a Black-headed Gull there, too, you know." Why Jeremiah has suddenly become such an optimist, I don't know. But I have noticed that the farther away we are from any bird, the more certain Hugh is we will see it. It is only as we approach the area that he begins to realize that the chances of success are nugatory.

When we reach Fort Erie, the Black-headed Gull is, of course, nowhere to be found, though, as always, we meet people who had it right under their feet yesterday and the day before that. One guy keeps saying this is a hard bird to miss. I do not suggest that he shut his cakehole before I do it for him. Fortunately, I am unarmed. This is the second time I have missed this bird. I do not know that I shall miss it again with Margaret and yet again with Hugh. They were "garbage birds" in England when I was there in January.

Daunted, but not yet completely broken, Hugh says, "Okay, let's go for Purple Sand." I see the beginning of dark depression hovering in the wings.

To pick up his spirits, I suggest we hit Tim Hortons at Chippewa to get the sandwich and soup combo, a doughnut, and coffee. The *Reisefuehrer*'s countenance brightens instantly. I know the soup and sandwich combo is his favourite lunch in the whole world. I learned that once when I proposed dropping into an exquisite little bakery café with lovely sandwiches and espresso coffee.

Hugh was mystified. "But there's a Tim Hortons just up ahead," he said in disbelief.

"Oh, well, say no more," I replied.

In post-Hortonic euphoria, sadly destined to be short-lived, Hugh says, "Let's go get that Purple. I know right where it's going to be on the rocks." The double Boston cream sometimes does this to him. You know, and I know, the bird is not going to be there, but you have to go and look.

It's not there. Nor do we find Little Gull. The *Reisefuehrer* is devastated. He feels betrayed, especially by the Little Gull. When it comes to optimism, the distance between the apogee and the nadir is scant with Hugh. "If we miss Little at Queenston, we'll have to do the flyby," he says sadly.

"No problem," I say.

We miss Little Gull at Queenston. It is cold and wet and late when we arrive at Niagara-on-the-Lake for the flyby. Significantly, there is no one else there and we tough it out till dark. Not even very many Bonaparte's go by. "The word must have got out we were coming," says Hugh bitterly. I have to take him into another Tim Hortons on the way home or I won't feel right leaving him alone later. Hugh does not get a single new bird today. "That's it for my three hundred," he says sadly. I feel guilty about the Hawk Owl and play it down. Just a lousy old Hawk Owl, even if it was 301.

Almost two weeks later I am still at 301. It is harder to motivate myself and little of interest is turning up on Ontbirds, except, of course, that damn Black-headed Gull. Then the King Eiders begin to show up again and Hugh and I are off. It's Mr. Toad all over again. Hugh thinks we have a pretty good chance of finally connecting with the gull and maybe even the eider. Or at least he does until Burlington. As we draw near Gray Road, he says, "Not much chance, really. The wind's wrong, the light's no good, and there are no other birders around." We try and fail.

We go to Sayers Park in a pathetic display of false optimism. Hugh doesn't even have a scope. It's in California being fixed after he dropped it hard on the pavement for the hundredth time. I'd love to be there when they open it. It reminds me of the Tilley hat that went through the elephant. Kowa should pick up on this and feature Hugh and his scope in their ads. They would have to be without sound; when his scope hits the pavement he sometimes says very ungentlemanly things. I have never been able to see anything out of it when I look. Anyway, we get out at Sayers and as I'm setting up my scope, Hugh says, "I've got a not bad candidate for eider." I look where he's pointing, swing my scope around, and bingo! — a pair of female **King Eiders** (302). Another brilliant beginning.

Unfortunately, we do not pay heed to Pope's Corollary Number 1 to Beadle's First Law: If you score a brilliant success right at the beginning, expect to pay dearly for that tiny bit of fun the whole rest of the day. Instead of going home, we rush around vainly searching for Black-headed Gull and Little Gull. Neither of us can believe we can't get Little Gull. It's the first year in ages that either of us has missed it. I should have chased it at McLaughlin Bay in May with Margaret when there were a few birds there, flying around in disbelief and despair that their wonderful adjacent habitat had been ruined. They have improved Oshawa Second Marsh to the point that there are hardly any Little Gulls at all — no mean feat of management as you could see 150 there three years ago and it was the best place in all of North America to find this gull. The bird is now best sought on Lake Erie, which is a bit far for me to go often. Richard Joos kindly offers to take me out to distant secret Little Gull haunts on Christmas morning, but I am otherwise occupied. I don't even run it by Felicity for a response.

I sense this makes a negative impression on Richard, who had up to this point struggled to believe I was a real birder. This bird eludes me in 2007.

But it's still 302 seen, 304 including heard-onlys. I don't have to horse trade on New Year's Eve.

20

The Big Dipper

Man's life is a cheat and a disappointment.

— THE FOUR TEMPTERS IN
MURDER IN THE CATHEDRAL BY T.S. ELIOT

Screw Dickcissel!

— HUGH CURRIE

No, THIS CHAPTER IS NOT about the celestial ramifications of ornithology. Nor is it about following the drinking gourd. I use it as a nominal metaphor, something like The Big Bopper — though the meaning in this latter case suggests a large person who bops. Big Dipper signifies a person, not necessarily large, who dips big time.

You will have noted that I have studiously avoided the verb "to dip" and the even more odious "dip out," used in England and Australia, throughout this text. Well, except for when Margaret missed the Ross's Goose and I couldn't resist it. I hate this use of the verb. Hughie talks about "dipping" all the time. It makes missing a bird seem even worse than it is.

I first heard the word used this way in Texas while looking at a Black-capped Vireo. The fellow who happened to be watching with me was as pleased as I was. "Yeaah, Ah'm pleased, too, re-aal pleased. Ah *dipped* on thet bird las' year," he opined. It somehow seemed awful to have a special verb for missing a bird. After this, I started hearing the word everywhere.

So, even though this chapter is about some of my more spectacular failures, frustrating misses, and soul-destroying disappointments, I shall eschew the verb *dip* and try to use English instead.

It all began with the bloody Razorbill. As soon as I got back from England in January, I rushed off to Niagara-on-the-Lake to try for the famous Razorbill, sensing it was about to disappear any day. When I arrived around 11:00 a.m. on a freezing, wet day near the end of the second week of January, as I made ready to go for the bird, I saw two cold, wet, bedraggled figures slowly and dejectedly wending their way across the golf course, obviously crushed and broken in spirit. As they drew near I saw it was Bob Curry and Glenda Slessor.

"Hey, Bob," I called cheerily. "Any luck?" I regretted my

question as I heard it issue from my mouth. They had obviously not seen the bird. They did not tell me to shut my festering gob before they did it for me. They are decent, soft-spoken people. But they must have thought it. Oh, yes. How could they help it? The Razorbill was obviously dozing in the swells off the east coast of Newfoundland if not being passed by a Gyrfalcon over Saint-Louis-du Ha! Ha! en route; the wind chill was vicious even without the driving sleet; and they were frozen stiff. Then some guy gets out of his warm vehicle with a large mug of coffee steaming like Mount Etna and asks, "Any luck?" I guess I had hoped they would say it was there, but you have to spend hours of suffering before getting a glimpse. But no, they had been there over four hours and had seen nothing. I offered condolences. No bird, but it saved me a lot of time. I figured if Bob and Glenda had not found it, there wasn't a snowball's chance in hell I was going to find it; so, I didn't even look, which means this was not even a full di—, I mean, miss. I think they call it a "demi-dip" in Texas; a "dipette" in Quebec.

When you chase a lot of birds hard, trying for some magical number, you're going to miss some — like the Townsend's Solitaire Margaret and I got so lost chasing in the Durham Regional Forest when attempting to make sense of a set of directions that our friends Rayfield Pye and Tyler Hoar had worked on together. It was our own fault for even dreaming these directions might actually lead us to the fowl.

I've told you about the birds I found. Now I shall tell you about a few more I missed. It would make the book too long to recount them all.

I told you about Little Gull — a classic case of "I'll get it later" syndrome, something to be avoided at all costs by Big Listers. You know how close I came to missing Eurasian Wigeon, Barred Owl, Sora, Eastern Screech-Owl, Acadian and Olive-sided Flycatcher, Louisiana Waterthrush, and King Eider. I am not even going to mention things like the Varied Thrush at Selkirk Provincial Park that betrayed me repeatedly and that I did not even expect to get.

But did I mention the Western Complex — birds whose names begin with the word Western? No, I did not. I have a strong dislike for almost all such birds. Take the Western Grebe, for example, a most unpleasant avian. I don't know how I could have loved them so much before 2007. The day after a Western was discovered on the Leslie Street Spit (even though there were those who felt at the time it might be a Clark's Grebe or a hybrid Clark's/Western), Andrew Don and I ran — literally — all the way to Pipit Point and combed the area. No Western Grebe. Carley, who had seen the bird and claimed he had "crippling views," feigned deep sympathy upon learning of my miss. Of course, the bird turned up again several days later and hung around until I could get there again, whereupon it went into deep hiding for the day. A month later another one turned up in Oakville but it, too, went AWOL when I went for it — twice. Andrew even got photos of this one, narrowly avoiding being attacked by it.

Then there is Western Sandpiper. There were not even very many to chase this year, but Margaret and I chased the few that were reported and missed the bird every time. Jean Iron saw one of the birds the day before and the day after Margaret and I chased it. This did not make me feel any better.

And how about Western Tanager and Western Wood-Pewee? I missed the tanager at Long Point and there was not even a whisper of Western Wood-Pewee at Rainy River where it has been found at least once. Speaking of Rainy River, I had high hopes of Western Kingbird out there and searched valiantly with zero luck.

And you wonder why I don't like birds with Western in their names. I make exception only for the Western Meadowlark, which broke ranks this year and presented itself widely and generously all over Rainy River — a noble fowl that saved me from destroying my first edition of Peterson's *A Field Guide to Western Birds*.

I mentioned nemesis birds earlier — birds used by the gods to punish cocksure birders, crush their over-weening pride and unwarranted confidence, and to generally make sure that one does not have any fun at all. Kentucky Warbler hardly counts here. I only missed it in one place — granted, four days in a row and always only by minutes — but this simply qualifies as run-of-the-mill disappointment. I could use Whip-poor-will as an example, but even here, although I missed it repeatedly everywhere, even for my heard-only list, I did not go hundreds of miles many times only to fail abjectly.

My real nemesis bird this year was the Dickcissel. Margaret got one at Pelee, so I could not even co-opt her into the search. Hugh, however, *needed* one and was determined to get me one, as well. I missed the first one posted by Geoff Carpentier north of Cobourg, but this was close to home and to be expected. Besides, nobody else found it. After several more misses, Hugh

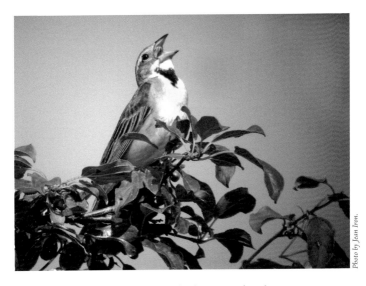

Photo by Jean Iron.

Dickcissel. Sanford. I saw this very bird in 2006, but the species managed to elude me during my Big Year.

phoned and said, "We gotta go to Ferndale in the Bruce if we're going to get Dickcissel."

Okay. It's a good five-hour drive from my home, but if we gotta go, we gotta go. They've been widely seen and reported and we have directions to the exact uncut fields where they have been seen.

We arrive and search for the main uncut field, which was literally swarming with Dickcissels just days before. We search diligently for the correct spot, and I wander down the road in the direction of some long grass, where I see some fairly rough-looking boys staring back at me. I think of the Carden

Alvar Birding Area and the generous spirit of some of the local farmers: "You lookin' in my field, Buddy? You like it I looked in your house windows at home?" Et cetera. One of the bigger men climbs the fence and walks right up to me. Trembling, I stand my ground on the shoulder. I plan to use the Norm Murr defence: "This road is public property. You can't kick me off it."

The guy walks right up to me and says, "You lookin' for them Dickcissels?"

"Ah, yeah, actually," I manage in reply.

"I had to cut the grass last week and haven't seen one since. But you're welcome to tramp around lookin' if you like. Might find 'em in the back forty. I ain't cut it yet. Nice bird, eh?"

A sterling chap. You never can tell. I recall a story by Kenn Kaufman called "Hell's Birders" in *Birdwatcher's Digest 22, No. 1* (September/October 1999), when he was suddenly surrounded by a hostile-looking leather-bedecked gang of motorcyclists who looked like they meant business. They did; they turned out to be keen birders.

Hugh and I search the back four thousand and every other possible place within miles of Ferndale — no Dickcissel, not even a call. It is not one of those magical Zen moments like when Peter Matthiessen fails to see the Snow Leopard. Nor do we experience the philosophical detachment of Kenn Kaufman when he fails to see the Harpy Eagle. Rather, we are crushed and I spend the drive home riding with a zombie. The *Reisefuehrer* has decided once again to give up birding and stick to Scrabble. Even Hortons' soup and sandwich combo fails to work its usual magic on him. I arrive back home after a seventeen-hour round trip. Felicity knows better than to ask. She pulls the cork and passes me a wine glass — a solace in my old age.

Someone posts Dickcissel again in Ferndale, right where we were. I phone Hugh. "Screw Dickcissel," he says bitterly. It's too early to entice him again.

That evening there is another posting. The phone rings. Mr. Toad syndrome has struck. "We can't miss them this time. I know exactly where to go. There are four places. We'll get 'em."

Sure, Hugh.

We go. We go everywhere. No Dickcissel.

"I would have been glad even to get one for my heard-only list," I sigh.

"The Dickcissel didn't say 'dick,'" says Hugh morosely. He decides to give up birding, this time definitively. I spend a pile on him in Tim Hortons. He never wants to hear about Dickcissels again.

Several days later Norm Murr goes to Ferndale and gets Dickcissel. I am afraid to phone Hugh. Unbeknownst to me, Hugh phones Norm and gets exact directions. My phone rings. "I know the exact place where Norm got it. It's a big field full of buffalo. The bird'll probably hang around since they won't cut this field. It's pasture. We're likely to get it. How often can you miss?"

I don't answer that question.

In disbelief, I find myself heading for the third and last time to Ferndale. We don't even find the buffalo. I hope they were all slaughtered, the bastards.

You want dipping, *that's* dipping.

21

Go Figure

It's a mug's game.

— LEFTIE CURRIE

I'VE BEEN RETHINKING MY BIG YEAR of late. Three hundred and two birds seen — 304 counting heard-onlys. According to Larry Neily's *Canadian Listers' Corner*, 2008 edition, no one else in any province in Canada broke three hundred last year except Margaret (301). Hugh was next with 297. And yet I missed almost two weeks while in England in early January, two weeks in Trinidad and Tobago, and two weeks on non-birding trips in Algonquin and Haliburton — actually six weeks in all. It seems hardly fair when missing these six weeks was not my fault. To level the playing field, we really have to pro-rate my number of birds seen over forty-six weeks instead of fifty-two. Then, of course, there's my handicap based on it being the first time I've done Big Year. And away with age-related discrimination! It's time to start talking about the senior citizen's bonus and pro-rating according to age, to say nothing of compensation for the birds missed when my telescope was out of commission for a full week. Let us not forget the two-bird grandchild allotment, since my grandchildren were here for weeks on end. Let us also not forget that I've lost 5 percent of my hearing. As Bruce Falls says, "Any fool can identify a Black-throated Green Warbler if

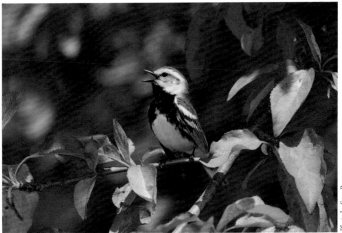

Photo by Sam Barone.

Black-throated Green Warbler (male). Red Bay, north of Wiarton. Beak wide open, this male is doing his best to be heard.

you hear it sing, *Zee zee zee ZEEE zoo zee*. But it takes a real man to identify it if all you hear is one tentative, whispered *zee*.

Away with all unfair prejudices! I'm for peace, freedom for the oppressed, and levelling the playing field. Of course, unlike others who shan't be mentioned, I refused all steroids and related drugs and staunchly refused blood-doping and testosterone shots, though, of course, unfortunately this doesn't get me any credits. I also get no credits for having the bad luck to pick a year when millions were not killed in deadly hurricanes with propitious winds for Ontario; nary a petrel, shearwater, or rare tern all fall. Coady had hurricanes coming out the yin-yang in '96 and millions died. Some people have all the luck. Where, I ask, were the hurricane Frans of 2007? In all but two states, according to ABA rules, I would get at least a five-bird allowance for such bad luck; but not in Ontario.

It goes without saying that I get a couple of birds in compensation for habitat loss. I mentioned how Oshawa Second Marsh was improved so as to become obviously repulsive to Little Gulls. This was also the year our beloved Corner Marsh was improved right out of existence. I guess I should consider myself lucky that they have not yet improved the Leslie Street Spit to this degree. They certainly are trying.

When I graphed it all out and did the figures on a calculator according to the principles of higher calculus and quantum theory, rounding down to the nearest full figure — to my disadvantage though this might be — it came out to 339, even without the five-bird hurricane handicap. It took some time to sink in that, in actual fact, I had whupped Coady, soundly for that matter, whupped him good, and was the new world record holder for the highest number of birds in one year in Ontario.

I neither ask nor expect to be carried through the streets laurel-bedecked on a litter of gold. I expect to be shunned and spat upon like so many winners in the past — Copernicus and Galileo spring immediately to mind, not to mention Genghis Khan, General Amin, and Pope Joan. A prophet in his own land is always without honour. My only satisfaction lies in knowing that I am the true record-holder, the king, the "onliest," even if only clandestinely and unacknowledged.

Ainsi soit-il.

Appendix 1:

Lists of Birds

January

+   Canada Goose. January 10, Cobourg Harbour
+   American Black Duck. January 10, Cobourg Harbour
+   Mallard. January 10, Cobourg Harbour
+   Greater Scaup. January 10, Cobourg Harbour
+   Long-tailed Duck. January 10, Cobourg Harbour
+   Common Merganser. January 10, Cobourg Harbour
+   Ring-billed Gull. January 10, Cobourg Harbour
+   Herring Gull. January 10, Cobourg Harbour

- Mourning Dove. January 10, Cobourg
- House Sparrow. January 10, Cobourg
- Bufflehead. January 11, Cobourg Harbour
- Common Goldeneye. January 11, Cobourg Harbour
- California Gull. January 11, Hamilton
- Mute Swan. January 11, Niagara-on-the-Lake
- White-winged Scoter. January 11, Niagara-on-the-Lake
- Hooded Merganser. January 11, Niagara-on-the-Lake
- Red-breasted Merganser. January 11, Niagara-on-the-Lake
- Red-throated Loon. January 11, Niagara-on-the-Lake
- Double-crested Cormorant. January 11, Niagara-on-the-Lake
- Great Blue Heron. January 11, Niagara-on-the-Lake
- Blue Jay. January 11, Niagara-on-the-Lake
- American Crow. January 11, Niagara-on-the-Lake
- Thayer's Gull. January 11, Niagara River (Adam Beck)
- Iceland Gull. January 11, Niagara River (Adam Beck)
- Glaucous Gull. January 11, Niagara River (Adam Beck)
- Great Black-backed Gull. January 11, Niagara River (Adam Beck)
- Black-legged Kittiwake. January 11, Niagara River (Adam Beck)
- Rock Pigeon. January 11, Niagara River (Adam Beck)
- Red-tailed Hawk. January 11, Niagara River (Adam Beck)
- American Kestrel. January 11, Niagara River (Adam Back area)
- Bonaparte's Gull. January 11, Niagara River (Adam Beck)
- Black-capped Chickadee. January 11, Niagara Falls
- Northern Mockingbird. January 11, Niagara Falls
- European Starling. January 11, Niagara Falls
- Lesser Black-backed Gull. January 11, Niagara River (above Falls)
- Downy Woodpecker. January 11, Chippewa
- Tufted Titmouse. January 11, Chippewa
- White-breasted Nuthatch. January 11, Chippewa

Appendix 1: List of Birds

- White-throated Sparrow. January 11, Chippewa
- Dark-eyed Junco. January 11, Chippewa
- House Finch. January 11, Chippewa
- American Goldfinch. January 11, Chippewa
- Tundra Swan. January 11, Niagara River
- Gadwall. January 11, Niagara River
- Canvasback. January 11, Niagara River

- American Coot. January 13, Cobourg Harbour

- Common Raven. January 14, Northumberland County Forest
- Red-breasted Nuthatch. January 14, Northumberland County Forest
- Red Crossbill. January 14, Northumberland County Forest
- White-winged Crossbill. January 14, Northumberland County Forest

- Hairy Woodpecker. January 19, Algonquin Provincial Park (Algonquin)
- Gray Jay. January 19, Algonquin
- American Tree Sparrow. January 19, Algonquin
- Purple Finch. January 19, Algonquin
- Pine Siskin. January 19, Algonquin
- Evening Grosbeak. January 19, Algonquin
- Common Redpoll. January 19, Algonquin (Spruce Bog Trail)

- Ruffed Grouse. January 20, Algonquin
- Boreal Chickadee. January 20, Algonquin (Opeongo Road)
- Black-backed Woodpecker. January 20, Algonquin (Opeongo Road)

- American Three-toed Woodpecker. January 21, Algonquin (Spruce Bog Trail)
- Spruce Grouse. January 21, Algonquin (Spruce Bog Trail)
- Northern Shrike. January 21, Roseneath
- Northern Cardinal. January 21, Cobourg (Margaret's Feeders)

- Rough-legged Hawk. January 22, Cobourg

- Redhead. January 23, Presqu'ile Provincial Park (Presqu'ile)
- American Robin. January 23, Presqu'ile

- Snow Bunting. January 24, Port Hope (just north on Highway 28)

- American Wigeon. January 27, Kingston
- Northern Pintail. January 27, Kingston
- Ring-necked Duck. January 27, Kingston
- Northern Harrier. January 27, Kingston

- Horned Lark. January 29, Port Hope (Dickinson Road)
- Lapland Longspur. January 29, Port Hope (Dickinson Road)

- Barrow's Goldeneye. January 30, Presqu'ile

January Total: 75

February

- Greater White-fronted Goose. February 18, Salem (Blyth Park Road)

Appendix 1: List of Birds

- Horned Grebe. February 23, Humber Bay
- Short-eared Owl. February 23, Fisherville
- Red-bellied Woodpecker. February 23, Selkirk Provincial Park

- Ring-necked Pheasant. February 25, Amherst Island
- Snowy Owl. February 25, Amherst Island
- Long-eared Owl. February 25, Amherst Island
- Northern Saw-whet Owl. February 25, Amherst Island

- Cooper's Hawk. February 27, Prince Edward County
- Harris's Sparrow. February 27, Prince Edward County

- Wild Turkey. February 28, Peterborough Airport

February Total: 11   Running Total: 86

March

- Laughing Gull. March 5, Cobourg Harbour

- Wood Duck. March 12, Ashbridge's Bay
- Red-winged Blackbird. March 12, Ashbridge's Bay
- Common Grackle. March 12, Ashbridge's Bay
- Red-necked Grebe. March 12, Leslie Street Spit
- Surf Scoter. March 12, Gray Road
- Black Scoter. March 12, Gray Road
- Gray Partridge. March 12, Brantford Airport

- Green-winged Teal. March 14, Cobourg Harbour

- Ruddy Duck. March 14, Cobourg Harbour
- Harlequin Duck. March 14, Cobourg (Lucas Point)
- Song Sparrow. March 14, Cobourg (Lucas Point)

- Brown-headed Cowbird. March 18, Wicklow

- Snow Goose. March 19, Cobourg Harbour

- Lesser Scaup. March 20, Cobourg Harbour

- Northern Shoveler. March 22, Long Point
- Pied-billed Grebe. March 22, Long Point
- Turkey Vulture. March 22, Long Point
- Bald Eagle. March 22, Long Point
- Sandhill Crane. March 22, Long Point
- Killdeer. March 22, Long Point
- Northern Flicker. March 22, Long Point
- Tree Swallow. March 22, Long Point
- Eastern Bluebird. March 22, Long Point
- Eastern Towhee. March 22, Long Point
- Fox Sparrow. March 22, Long Point
- Eastern Meadowlark. March 22, Long Point
- Rusty Blackbird. March 22, Long Point

- American Woodcock. March 26, Grafton (Thomas Road)
- Great Horned Owl. March 26, Grafton (Thomas Road)
- Pileated Woodpecker. March 26, Cobourg

- Eastern Phoebe. March 27, Thickson's Woods

Appendix 1: List of Birds

+ Red-shouldered Hawk. March 30, Wilberforce

March Total: 33   Running Total: 119

April

+ Eared Grebe. April 2, Grimsby Sewage Lagoons
+ Forster's Tern. April 2, Port Rowan
+ Blue-winged Teal. April 2, Long Point
+ Brown Creeper. April 2, Long Point
+ Winter Wren. April 2, Long Point
+ Golden-crowned Kinglet. April 2, Long Point
+ Field Sparrow. April 2, Long Point

+ Hermit Thrush. April 3, Cobourg (Margaret's Backyard)
+ White-crowned Sparrow. April 3, Cobourg (Margaret's Backyard)

+ Osprey. April 9, Buckhorn

+ Common Loon. April 12, Bronte

+ Sharp-shinned Hawk. April 13, Toronto

+ Wilson's Snipe. April 14, Cobourg (Normar Road)
+
+ Yellow-bellied Sapsucker. April 15, Lynde Shores
  Conservation Area
+ Swamp Sparrow. April 15, Lynde Shores Conservation Area

+ Greater Yellowlegs. April 21, Reesor Pond

- Barn Swallow. April 21, Corner Marsh
- Cedar Waxwing. April 21, Cranberry Marsh
- Belted Kingfisher. April 21, Thickson's Woods
- Ruby-crowned Kinglet. April 21, Thickson's Woods

- Yellow-rumped Warbler. April 24, Cobourg (my backyard)

- Caspian Tern. April 25, Presqu'ile
- Purple Martin. April 25, Presqu'ile
- Northern Rough-winged Swallow. April 25, Presqu'ile
- Brown Thrasher. April 25, Presqu'ile
- Pine Warbler. April 25, Presqu'ile
- Palm Warbler. April 25, Presqu'ile
- Chipping Sparrow. April 25, Presqu'ile

- Savannah Sparrow. April 26, Baillieborough

- Chimney Swift. April 27, Stoney Creek (Edgewater)
- Blue-headed Vireo. April 27, Stoney Creek (Edgewater)
- Yellow-throated Warbler. April 27, Stoney Creek (Edgewater)
- Broad-winged Hawk. April 27, Hamilton
- Black-throated Green Warbler. April 27, Thickson's Woods

- American Bittern. April 28, Leslie Street Spit
- Great Egret. April 28, Leslie Street Spit
- Black-crowned Night-Heron. April 28, Leslie Street Spit
- Spotted Sandpiper. April 28, Leslie Street Spit
- Common Tern. April 28, Leslie Street Spit
- Bank Swallow. April 28, Leslie Street Spit
- Cliff Swallow. April 28, Leslie Street Spit

Appendix 1: List of Birds

- Cape May Warbler. April 28, Leslie Street Spit
- Black-throated Blue Warbler. April 28, Leslie Street Spit
- Black-and-white Warbler. April 28, Leslie Street Spit

- Lesser Yellowlegs. April 29, Nonquon Sewage Lagoons
- Least Sandpiper. April 29, Nonquon Sewage Lagoons

April Total: 46   Running Total: 165

May

- Marbled Godwit. May 1, Amherst Island
- Pectoral Sandpiper. May 1, Amherst Island
- Wilson's Phalarope. May 1, Amherst Island

- Ruby-throated Hummingbird. May 4, Thickson's Woods
- Wood Thrush. May 4, Thickson's Woods
- Nashville Warbler. May 4, Thickson's Woods
- Ovenbird. May 4, Thickson's Woods
- Rose-breasted Grosbeak. May 4, Thickson's Woods

- House Wren. May 5, Thickson's Woods
- Gray Catbird. May 5, Thickson's Woods
- Veery. May 5, Thickson's Woods
- Swainson's Thrush. May 5, Thickson's Woods
- Northern Parula. May 5, Thickson's Woods
- Magnolia Warbler. May 5, Thickson's Woods
- American Redstart. May 5, Thickson's Woods
- Lincoln's Sparrow. May 5, Thickson's Woods
- Baltimore Oriole. May 5, Thickson's Woods

- Least Flycatcher. May 7, Rondeau Provincial Park
- Yellow Warbler. May 7, Rondeau Provincial Park
- Chestnut-sided Warbler. May 7, Rondeau Provincial Park
- Cerulean Warbler. May 7, Rondeau Provincial Park
- Common Yellowthroat. May 7, Rondeau Provincial Park
- Black-bellied Plover. May 7, Hillman's Marsh
- Semipalmated Plover. May 7, Hillman's Marsh
- Dunlin. May 7, Hillman's Marsh
- Short-billed Dowitcher. May 7, Hillman's Marsh
- Warbling Vireo. May 7, Hillman's Marsh
- American Pipit. May 7, Hillman's Marsh

- American Golden-Plover. May 8, Hillman's Marsh
- Red-headed Woodpecker. May 8, Point Pelee
- Great Crested Flycatcher. May 8, Point Pelee
- Eastern Kingbird. May 8, Point Pelee
- White-eyed Vireo. May 8, Point Pelee
- Blue-gray Gnatcatcher. May 8, Point Pelee
- Blackburnian Warbler. May 8, Point Pelee
- Bay-breasted Warbler. May 8, Point Pelee
- Worm-eating Warbler. May 8, Point Pelee
- Northern Waterthrush. May 8, Point Pelee
- Hooded Warbler. May 8, Point Pelee
- Wilson's Warbler. May 8, Point Pelee
- Summer Tanager. May 8, Point Pelee
- Scarlet Tanager. May 8, Point Pelee
- Grasshopper Sparrow. May 8, Point Pelee
- Henslow's Sparrow. May 8, Point Pelee
- Indigo Bunting. May 8, Point Pelee
- Orchard Oriole. May 8, Point Pelee

Appendix 1: List of Birds

- Philadelphia Vireo. May 9, Point Pelee
- Carolina Wren. May 9, Point Pelee
- Marsh Wren. May 9, St. Clair Wildlife Area
- Yellow-headed Blackbird. May 9, Angler Line
- Prairie Warbler. May 9, Point Pelee
- Canada Warbler. May 9, Point Pelee

- Black Tern. May 10, Pelee Marsh Boardwalk
- Black-billed Cuckoo. May 10, Point Pelee
- Eastern Wood-Pewee. May 10, Point Pelee
- Red-eyed Vireo. May 10, Point Pelee
- Blue-winged Warbler. May 10, Point Pelee
- Tennessee Warbler. May 10, Point Pelee
- Mourning Warbler. May 10, Point Pelee

- Solitary Sandpiper. May 11, Pelee Island
- Bobolink. May 11, Pelee Island

- Blackpoll Warbler. May 12, Pelee Island

- Common Moorhen. May 13, Pelee Island

- Green Heron. May 14, Pelee Island
- Virginia Rail. May 14, Pelee Island

- Yellow-billed Cuckoo. May 15, Pelee Island

- American Avocet. May 16, Hillman's Marsh
- White-rumped Sandpiper. May 16, Hillman's Marsh
- Yellow-bellied Flycatcher. May 16, Rondeau Provincial Park

+ Prothonotary Warbler. May 16, Rondeau Provincial Park

+ Sedge Wren. May 19, Presqu'ile

+ Brant. May 23, Nonquon Sewage Lagoons
+ Semipalmated Sandpiper. May 23, Nonquon Sewage Lagoons

+ Whimbrel. May 24, Colonel Sam Smith Park
+ Willow Flycatcher. May 24, Colonel Sam Smith Park
+ Gray-cheeked Thrush. May 24, Colonel Sam Smith Park

+ Upland Sandpiper. May 25, Carden Alvar (Wylie Road)
+ Common Nighthawk. May 25, Carden Alvar (Alvar Road)
+ Loggerhead Shrike. May 25, Carden Alvar (Wylie Road)
+ Vesper Sparrow. May 25, Carden Alvar (Wylie Road)

+ Merlin. May 26, Kirkfield
+ Clay-colored Sparrow. May 26, Carden Alvar (Cameron Ranch)

+ Yellow-throated Vireo. May 29, Opinicon Road
+ Golden-winged Warbler. May 29, Opinicon Road
+ Alder Flycatcher (Number 250). May 29, Northumberland County (Stoney Point Road)

May Total: 85   Running Total: 250

Appendix 1: List of Birds

June

- Ruddy Turnstone. June 1, Cobourg Harbour

- Cattle Egret. June 4, Gasline
- Lark Sparrow. June 4, Long Point
- Louisiana Waterthrush. June 4, Long Point

- Least Bittern. June 13, Lone Pine Marsh

- Brewer's Blackbird. June 15, Desbarats

- American White Pelican. June 17, Rainy River Road
- Sharp-tailed Grouse. June 17, Rainy River Road
- Black-billed Magpie. June 17, Rainy River Road
- Western Meadowlark. June 17, Rainy River
- Franklin's Gull. June 17, Rainy River
- Piping Plover. June 18, Windy Point
- Le Conte's Sparrow. June 20, Fred's Marsh

June Total: 13   Running Total: 263

July

- Northern Goshawk. July 6, Kilbride

- Barred Owl. July 16, Straggle Lake

- Eurasian Collared-Dove. July 20, Stoney Creek
- Acadian Flycatcher. July 20, Spooky Hollow

- Stilt Sandpiper. July 20, Jarvis Sewage Lagoons

- Sanderling. July 26, Cobourg Harbour

July Total: 6   Running Total: 269

August

- Baird's Sandpiper. August 19, Presqu'ile
- Red-necked Phalarope. August 19, Nonquon Sewage Lagoons
- Willet. August 19, Cranberry Marsh

- Olive-sided Flycatcher. August 26, Cobourg
- Long-billed Dowitcher. August 26, Brighton Water Polishing Facility

- Red Knot. August 27, Presqu'ile

August Total: 6   Running Total: 275

September

- Buff-breasted Sandpiper. September 8, Beeton Sod Farms
- Sabine's Gull. September 8, Van Wagner's Beach
-
- Eastern Screech-Owl. September 18, Cobourg

- Ruff. September 19, Harrington

September Total: 4   Running Total: 279

Appendix 1: List of Birds

October

* Peregrine Falcon. October 3, Presqu'ile Provincial Park
* Parasitic Jaeger. October 3, Presqu'ile Provincial Park

* Nelson's Sharp-tailed Sparrow. October 4, Cootes Paradise

* Golden Eagle. October 9, Prince Edward Point

* Cackling Goose. October 11, Lynde Shores Conservation Area

* Orange-crowned Warbler. October 12, Hillman's Marsh

* Sora. October 14, Pelee Marsh Boardwalk
* Northern Wheatear. October 14, Shrewsbury

* Hudsonian Godwit. October 15, Coot's Pond (Darlington)

* Pomarine Jaeger. October 16, Van Wagner's Beach

* White-faced Ibis. October 20, Cootes Pond (Hamilton)

* Ross's Goose. October 23, Reesor Pond

* Trumpeter Swan. October 28 (Okayed by OBRC), Cobourg Harbour

* Eurasian Wigeon. October 29, Kingston

October Total: 14   Running Total: 293

November

- Pacific Loon. November 3, Lake Ontario off Oshawa Second Marsh

- Bohemian Waxwing. November 4, Willow Beach (Lake Simcoe)

- Pine Grosbeak. November 20, Brighton

- Yellow-breasted Chat. November 21, Ashbridge's Bay
- Northern Gannet. November 21, Cobourg Harbour

November Total: 5   Running Total: 298

December

- Hoary Redpoll. December 4, Margaret's Backyard
- **Purple Sandpiper (Number 300)**. December 4, Presqu'ile (Gull Island)

- Northern Hawk Owl. December 10, Stoney Creek

- King Eider. December 22, Sayers Park

December Total: 4   **Grand Total of Birds Seen: 302**

Appendix 1: List of Birds

BIRDS I ONLY HEARD IN 2007

- King Rail. June 16, Pumpkin Point Marsh
- Connecticut Warbler. June 20, Rainy River
- [Northern Bobwhite. June 4, Long Point; not countable]

Total: 2   **Grand Total of Birds Seen and Heard: 304**

BIRDS I EXPECTED TO SEE BUT DID NOT SEE IN 2007

- Western Grebe
- Tricolored Heron
- Western Sandpiper
- Red Phalarope
- Long-tailed Jaeger
- Little Gull
- Great Gray Owl
- Boreal Owl
- Rufous Hummingbird
- Whip-poor-will
- Townsend's Solitaire
- Varied Thrush
- Kirtland's Warbler
- Kentucky Warbler
- Dickcissel

Birds I Felt I Had a Good Chance to See But Did Not See in 2007

- Tufted Duck
- Common Eider
- Great Cormorant
- Snowy Egret
- Yellow-crowned Night-Heron
- Glossy Ibis
- Black Vulture
- Gyrfalcon
- Black-headed Gull
- Arctic Tern
- Western Kingbird
- Cave Swallow

Birds I Did See, But Did Not Think I Had a Good Chance to See

- White-faced Ibis
- Sabine's Gull
- Eurasian Collared-Dove
- Northern Wheatear
- Lark Sparrow

(I had hoped this category would be larger.)

Best Bird of the Year

- Northern Wheatear

Acknowledgements

No man is an island, or even a peninsula, entire of itself.

— Jon Dunne, his only *Meditation*

When you do a Big Year, you don't do it alone; you need help. All birders will know people similar to my two main accomplices. Actually, probably not, come to think of it. What I meant to say is that they will know people who play the same roles for them in their birding endeavours as my two partners did.

It would be churlish not to thank Hugh Currie up front for conceiving the idea in the first place that I should do a Big Year in Ontario. Though he led me to the slaughter not entirely without deceit, it would be pusillanimous not to acknowledge his leading role. I could have had a worse mentor; he has seen over three hundred in a year in Ontario more than once and his all-time Ontario life list is 418 as of this writing. One doesn't get that number of birds without knowing something about where and how to find them. His philosophy is that the one who stays home by the phone or the computer gets the most birds in the long run; he doesn't like "fishing trips" or going about aimlessly looking for birds. He likes to wait for leads on twitchable birds and then rush off in hot pursuit. He saw 297 in Ontario this year in spite of a manic predisposition to Scrabble and bridge, and a four-week trip to Peru (which put him over five thousand on his world list) at a crucial time in the fall. He's a serious birder — a twitcher. Rigid, compulsive, and obsessive others might say, but you need someone like this. It should perhaps be mentioned that in these pages he is occasionally referred to as the *Reisefuehrer* or trip leader, albeit with a touch of *lèse majesté*.

Then, of course, there's my other main partner in crime, Margaret Bain, former Chair of the Ontario Bird Records Committee — a presence. Margaret is what is usually called, perhaps euphemistically, "a going concern." She has the biggest backyard list in all of Cobourg, and perhaps Ontario. (It includes Kirtland's Warbler!) She volunteered to help — or did I dragoon her, I forget — and to feed me birds. I figured from the start that if I could stay ahead of her, I'd have a pretty good chance at three hundred. The difficulty of such a manoeuvre was what pushed me over the top. Margaret, it should be mentioned, is not averse to "fishing trips" and likes to tear around and find her own birds. She ended up with 301 birds for the year. Not bad for someone who claimed for ever so long that she wasn't really trying at all to stay even with me, let alone, God forbid, ahead of me.

Many others deserve my thanks, including the redoubtable Jim Fairchild, who, sadly, passed away shortly before publication doing the very thing he loved (it was always hard to stay ahead of this one; no matter how hot and secret the tip you had just received, Jim would be there looking for the bird when you arrived); Doug McRae; Fred Helleiner (whom I have known since he was my camp counsellor when I was only eight years old — he has much to answer for); Andrew Don; Atikokan's own Dave Elder; Dan Lee; Don Shanahan; Cheryl Edgecombe and the Hamilton crew; Bruce Ripley and the Kingston crew; Willy and Betsy D'Anna and their fellow New Yorkers, the patrollers of the Niagara River who miss little (and people think those traffic jams on the Niagara bridges are caused by tourists and truckers); and people too numerous to be named who phoned me or posted good stuff on Ontbirds (the Ontario Field Ornithologists' listing site).

Bob Curry, Ron Pittaway, and Mark Peck never failed to ask me how my Big Year was going — quite a spur. The first person to congratulate me on reaching three hundred was Mark. I ran into him in a rather seedy tavern — an unexpected place to meet a senior ornithologist from the Royal Ontario Museum, to be sure. I believe I was there canvassing for some worthy charity — and he told me I had really achieved something. True, he seemed rather surprised, even bewildered, but it made the whole thing seem worthwhile to me.

Apart from repeatedly saying things like, "It will be nice to have a life again when this is over," my wife, Felicity, was a tower of strength during my Big Year, especially toward the end when she realized what it would be like to live with me if I only got to 299. She read a few of the early excerpts and commented that some of what I had written was mildly witty — in the parts that weren't just juvenile (or did she say sophomoric?). Anyway, for this keen encouragement, I am grateful. She was also the first to point out that much of the appeal of this book lies in the fact that readers will immediately realize that anybody can succeed in a Big Year if I did, although she did not spell out the last part.

I would like to thank and praise the photographers, fellow birders all, who so kindly and gladly let me use some of their brilliant work: Sam Barone (OFO and TOC), Jean Iron (OFO and TOC, digiscoper supreme), my birding buddy Andrew Don (OFO), Barry S. Cherriere (OFO), Mark Peck (ROM, OFO, TOC), Carol M. Horner (OFO, TOC), Doug McRae (OFO and a scamp), Steve Pike (OFO), and Mike Burrell (OFO). Their photography lifts the book up to a higher level. I badly wanted to avoid the sort of Karsh-type bird portraits that might be appropriate for a field guide or picture book of birds, and all of them came through for me. It might also be mentioned that, where possible, I chose pictures of the actual birds that I myself saw. Hal Bowen has once again proved his genius with a camera by getting a shot of me where I look borderline normal, something few other photographers, for some reason, have been able to do.

And then there are the artists: David Beadle and Neil Broadfoot. After we saw the Northern Wheatear together at Shrewsbury, I asked Dave to paint me a Wheatear for the cover and he produced the stunning picture that appears on the front of this book. Neil, a member of the Canadian Society of Painters in Water Colour who has illustrated two other books for me, did the maps and the other little impressionistic drawings in classic Broadfoot style. Thanks, guys.

Last, but far from least, I would like to thank Barry Penhale and Jane Gibson, Allison Hirst, Jennifer Scott, and Susan DeMille — Barry and Jane for their unflagging support of the book right from the start, Allison for her conscientious and thoughtful editorial work and for her attempts to keep me within the bounds, Jennifer for her inspired layout and design work, and Sue for her expert advice and help with the colour photographs.

Felicity Pope, Margaret Bain, Hugh Currie, and, of course, Allison Hirst, all read the text with an eye to various errors. If any errors remain, I just can't imagine to whom they should be attributed.

Parts of this book appeared in an earlier form in the *Newsletter* of the Toronto Ornithological Club under the excellent editorship of David Farrell. Club members' constant encouragement was much appreciated. Sandra Eadie appears to have found it killingly funny. She has soared in my estimation. I hope everyone responds to the book as she has.

It should perhaps be mentioned in closing that the use of capitalization for all specific bird names follows normal usage in the field and, as Kenn Kaufman's editor explains in a note at the outset of Kenn's classic *Kingbird Highway*, it allows one to avoid ambiguity; for example, Little Gulls refers to more than one Little Gull, whereas little gulls means the smaller species rather than the larger ones.

Index

Index

Index